Songs of the Night Skies:
A Grimoire of Healing, Empowerment and Justice

by Gianmichael Salvato

Dedication and Acknowledgments

This book is dedicated with inexpressible gratitude and love to my Ancestors, to my Tribe at the Inner Alchemy Mystery School, to my companions within the Contemplative Order of Compassion, and to my husband, Craig Daube.

Special thanks to the two beautiful souls who were contributors to the foreword and afterword of this book, Andrea Savar and Michael Thérèse McQueen respectively; and to Dan Mowery, Mary-Grace Fahrun, Dr. Debra Cannon, and to my baby sister, Jeanine Salvato-Wethal.

Finally, I dedicate this to the memories of my Dad, Francis Pietro Salvato, who will always be one of my greatest heroes and inspirations; and to my Mom, Cecilia Salvato, I miss you every single day of my life.

My most sincere desire is that you never doubt that you are loved and appreciated beyond measure, and have profoundly and deeply impacted by life, my magical practice and my heart in ways that can never be adequately repaid. I love you, and hope this book honours you.

About the Author

Gianmichael Salvato is a gender non-conforming (pronouns: they/them/their) author, naturopath, anthropologist, alchemist, intersectional feminist, Queer activist, herbalist, contemplative mystic and magical practitioner.

They are the founder of the Inner Alchemy Mystery School, and the Servant-Leader and Executive Director of the Contemplative Order of Compassion Sanctuary.

A lifelong practitioner of Italian and Afro-Sicilian folk magic, drawing on more than fifty years of personal study and lived experience, Gianmichael draws deeply from the well of Sacred Wisdom of the Ancestors and Spirits beyond the Veil, as well as from the esoteric Catholic and Franciscan mystical and contemplative traditions, New Thought philosophy and Hermeticism.

Gianmichael strives to live by these simple principles: personal responsibility, claiming one's own Power, speaking one's own Truth (at all costs), living that Truth , following no creed, and always maintaining and respecting Individual Sovereignty.

They live with their husband, Craig Daube, and continue to work toward the eventual building of a residential centre of co-creators according to the central guiding principles of the Contemplative Order of Compassion – a post-denominational, deconstructionist, secular humanist community of esoteric practitioners, social justice activists and humanitarians, founded in 1981.

Contents

Foreword

When my dear friend Gianmichael first told me of the project this book encapsulates, I gasped at the sheer volume of work it would entail. Unlike the many tomes churned out each year on the subjects of magical practice that leave the reader hollow of sustainable knowledge, this book is built on a lifetime of reflection and application.

There is a growing hunger for practice that is rooted in ancestral traditions without the pitfalls that can emerge from dividing ourselves into religious or social factions.

This book will most assuredly speak to those who have Italian heritage and always wondered why their grandmothers and grandfathers did some of the things they did in the garden, the kitchen, the late hours of Christmas Eve, in the whispers of grief or the joys of celebration. But it is written in such a way that those who are not Italian are invited to the table to feast on a meal that satiates the senses and fuels one's inner most abilities to see the magic in everything.

It is a book for humanity to remember the simplicity of the sacred.

Within this book are over fifty years of evolving study but I was immediately struck by the return to their early years and the first kindling of the magical fire within on many of the pages. I think we are all born with an innate ability to listen to the hum of the energy around us and see the dance of the spirits in the elements but slowly we forget the rhythms.

Gianmichael's journals create pathways that guide us on our own journey of remembering the words to a song of our ancestors and of the world around us. Each chapter is a reminder of how something as seemingly simple as sweeping the floor or stirring the Sunday gravy can be a revolutionary act of personal transformation and communal inspiration.

While our people NEVER would have referred to their ways as witchcraft or spells, these words are and were considered pejorative, for the sake of a common vernacular the book is beautifully organized as a book of secrets or teachings. It is a reflection on the methods used to shift the world around us in subtle ways that to the outsider can be hidden in plain sight but to those who know… well they know how effective the workings are.

This is not your typical rebranding of new age or neo-pagan practices; this is a book of the ways that folk magic healers have practiced in Italy (primarily Sicilian but also applicable to people like my family in the northern parts of Italy) for thousands of years.

There are historical references as well as personal revelations that do not rely on fabricated claims of fictitious origins. This is a book that truly delves into the heart of the ways that so many of our ancestors and modern-day practitioners see the intertwining of the natural world within our own bodies and our connection to one another.

I was honored to be asked to write this intro knowing the depth of knowledge that it contains and the roots that ground it. This is not a manual on how to call yourself a "*Strega*" (another term we do not generally use but that has become popular over the past decade) but rather a book on how to balance and remember the innate power within us and around us to connect to a holistic experience of the liminal. From honoring the days of the week to knitting healing into a scarf, there are practical applications that are subtle but potent.

There is also the intrinsic depth of knowledge that only comes from having lived a magical life in not only the glorious triumphs but also the soul crushing depths of loss. Gianmichael is not one to bite their tongue or conform to popularity contests, which is why this work is authentic in all the right ways.

I truly believe the timing of this book's release is also phenomenal considering the times we are living in and how they have deeply impacted the human psyche.

These teachings are a constellation of knowledge that shines bright even in the dark night of the soul humanity is experiencing. It is a way to gather the courage of our ancestors and combine them with an approach to life that is both grounding and respectful of the world around us and the beings within.

I am sure the success of this book is one that is not only intrinsic to the author but one that will ripple out infinitely to those who incorporate the methods to their own day to day life. Gianmichael's work reminds us that often the most magical thing one can do is to sweep the dust out the door, clean the kitchen counters, braid the garlic and share a cup of coffee with our ancestors.

It is a gift that I encourage all to partake in on this curious journey of a magical life.

Andrea Savar
Celebrated Author, Artisan, Mystic
www.AndreaSavar.com

CHAPTER ONE

As We Begin

"I learned that our tradition is very rich, and that it contains magical and religious rituals and prayers for the outward expression of our inner spirituality for every phase and condition of our lives… The practices of witchcraft, folk medicine, blessing rituals, cooking and crafting are inextricably woven into the fabric of Italian culture — no matter where Italians are geographically located."

Mary-Grace Fahrun
Author of *Italian Folk Magic: Rue's Kitchen Witchery*

Getting started using this grimoire, it might help to understand the perspective, worldview and practice of the author and my ancestors, upon whose traditions my own practice evolved.

My general sense is that those who consider themselves to be "white lighters", as well as those who embrace the notion that magical practice is not possible, unless one is initiated into and worships any particular deity, in any pantheon, will be put-off by this text, and with good reason. We don't share even a remotely common worldview, magical view or working philosophy.

Likewise, if you imagine that baneful work is "evil", or embrace the distorted, racist construct that considers there to be such a thing as "black magic" versus "white magic", then this is certainly not going to be a book that you will find resonant with your belief system.

Otherwise, there will be something of a universality within these pages, particularly reflective of my Afro-Sicilian heritage and magical tradition.

The island of Sicily, and by extension, the Southern Kingdom of Sicily (in what is now considered to be Southern Italy) has historically been a diverse, multi-cultural and ethnically-rich society, which has been under the rule of leaders from Africa, Greece, Spain, France, and other cultures, dating back over millennia. Even within the Common Era, we've seen the influences of the Norman conquest, Arab emirate rule, Roman conquests, French, Spanish, Maltese and other cultural influences that became part of the Sicilian culture.

Unlike many countries, in which nationalism and a singular identity played a rule in resistance to outside cultures in times of conquest, the Afro-Sicilian people demonstrate a fluidity that in itself is magical. As such, we integrate and incorporate into our way of life the best of the best from the many cultural influences that once found their homes on our island and its territories.

As a result of this, I grew up with a voracious appetite for wanting to understand those multi-cultural influences, especially as they related to the art, science and metaphysics of my ancestral home lands. And to that end, I would be raised to reject the notions of "black magic" versus "white magic" that was so popular in the neo-pagan and pop-culture religious witchcraft communities that were mobilising around the need to protect religious expression during the 1960s and 70s. I would (and still do) cringe at gatekeeping attempts, such as Laurie Cabot's "Witches Dos and Don'ts", while understanding that her likely intention was to diffuse some of the fears arising during the "Satanic Panic" mindset of the 1980s. And like my elders, I found the forced fusion of pagan revivalist interpretations of the old religions with secret society ritual and exaggerate interpretations of (mostly British) folk magic practices that became the bedrock of the American and European neo-pagan version of "witchcraft" to be fraught with problems from which I strongly wanted to remain disassociated.

Magical practice for me was something much more organic, unforced, and practical. And there would be differences, between the way that I practiced, compared to the elders who taught me our ways, and even from the cousins who were my contemporaries.

None of that seemed strange or threatening, and there was never a sense of "I'm right, and they're wrong," when those differences presented themselves.

For example, some of those closest to me are very attuned to the movement of the stars and the sun across the skies. Their astrological magic and insights are incredible to witness. But I never found any interest at all in those studies. My path was much more of a nocturnal path, guided and inspired by the lunar cycles, by working closely with nightshades and the shadow.

That didn't mean that I didn't work with or cultivate relationships with plants that grow by day, or that I was exclusively focused on baneful work. It simply meant that my studies would deepen my ability to harness those energies in the types of magic that would dominate most of my life's work.

It may be helpful to also understand that our tradition has existed for thousands of years before the creation of neo-pagan religious magical traditions, and so constructs like "casting a circle," or "calling the Quarters" are not necessarily foreign to me, as much as they are considered non-essential, and at times, more liturgical and theatrical than practical.

One of my students in recent years said that they would classify my approach to the esoteric and magical arts and sciences to be a synthesis of the world of television's *The Magicians* and the teen *Winx Saga*, combined with the approach of the aunts (and uncle) in Alice Hoffman's *Practical Magic* (and its subsequent prequel novels); instead of the pop-culture's approach that more closely resembles the 2015 classic film, The Coven, which is clearly inspired by Robert Cochrane's tradition of traditional British witchcraft. And that assessment is probably the most accurate one I've seen in a while.

So, when you read this book, know that the intention with which I compiled these spells and instructions was to provide the reader and practitioner with a useful framework, into which they could infuse their personal practice, tradition and customs. There's nothing that says you couldn't cast a circle, or invoke the deity or deities with whom you work before or during a particular working.

Whereas I might choose to do most of my workings at night, you might find that sitting in a brightly lit field, beside a sun-filled sky to be your most natural setting.

There's nothing necessarily nefarious or mystical behind my approach, by comparison to those who are "day workers". I simply find the quietude and energy of the night to be more stilling, less distracting, and richer with the essence and spirits of my ancestors, who were all about the "moon and water", being from an island in the Mediterranean, than let's say the Alpine Italians, who might have found resonance in the experience of earth and sky, during the daytime.

There is a song from the folk-traditions of Catholicism in the 1960s and 70s, which says, "What you hear in the dark, you must speak in the light..." and I think that captures the freedom with which I hope you will approach this grimoire:

Regardless of whether you prefer to work at night or by day, try to be mindful that there are seen and unseen energies at work, and expand your awareness to become mindful that once you're created the working itself, you've created something of an "anchor" to a point in time during which something far greater than the ritual took place, so that when you "let it go" to do its work, your words (in the daylight or mundane daily life) should reflect the confidence of an adept magical practitioner.

In our family tradition, the elders would often encourage that every esoteric practitioner keep journals, which we referred to as *i libri di segreti (Books of Secrets)*, somewhat analogous, I suppose, to Gardner's "Book of Shadows". The idea is that this book isn't intended to be a coffee table curiosity, or something that sits on the shelf to show how well-read you are. It's a workbook that is designed to inspire your own crafting of a book far more powerful and useful than anything any other author could draft, because it will be YOUR book of magic, of reflections, of observations and experimentation.

And that will guide you farther toward greater success than anything someone else could ever offer.

Mythology tells of a time when each family might have only one *libro di segreti*, which might be handed down from generation to generation, and there are in my possession, books which are claimed to be just that. However, I am a scientist and skeptic, and while some of these texts are written in old forms of *siciulo*, the Afro-Sicilian indigenous language, of which I am not fluent, other texts are in Southern dialects of Salernatino and Napolitano, which I had a much easier time understanding. And I can tell you than in none of the texts or journals, did it appear to me that these books were written with the intention of being the "sole handbook" for an entire family, the way that neo-pagan Books of Shadows would have been handed down to an entire religious coven.

Instead, they appear to be journals and notebooks, which surely would have been passed down, and maybe even shared among a practitioner's family, but not as a sole authority or codified handbook. For me, the existence of these journals and notebooks, which often demonstrate that two siblings, living at the same time and under the same roof, might have each had their own, provide us with insight into the experiential wisdom that each of us, as practitioners of the esoteric, have the potential to experience.

So please consider reading this with a journal or notebook yourself, as I ask my students at the Inner Alchemy Mystery School[1] to do.

---

[1] The Inner Alchemy Mystery School was founded in 1998, as a place for bringing together practitioners of folk magic from throughout the Mediterranean world. For more information, visit: www.InnerAlchemy.online

Introduction to the Italian Magical Worldview

Let's begin with a look at the Italian and Afro-Sicilian magical worldview.

From our perspective, we live in a world that is entirely magical, mystical and energetic. We see the cosmos itself as being intelligent and conscious. Therefore, even the things that might otherwise be thought of as mundane are, at the very least, subtle magic.

Our belief is that the experience of live teaches us how to master the skills of working with energy, both gross and subtle, and manipulating or shifting it to our will. That's why one would be hard-pressed to find someone in ancient Sicily or Italy, who called what they were doing "witchcraft" (*stregoneria*). In order to do so would mean that we believed what we were doing was something extraordinary, which only a few people could do. But our essential worldview is that each of us not only can, but *actually does* work magically, from the moment we're born.

We can observe this in children, around the world.

When a child wants something, they instinctively begin to work magically, shifting the energy around circumstances, people (especially people), objects and conditions, in order to make it possible for them to secure whatever it is they want.

Sometimes, they will begin by drawing themselves with whatever it is. (Sounds like working with sigils and symbols!) Other times, they may use something else, and pretend that it's the thing they want — perhaps a tree branch that resembles an airplane. (Correspondences, right?) And then there is the dreamwork, the statements of intention, and their persuasion over adults.

So, everything from the way we perceive the elements (and elementals), to the way we cook, clean and interact with the world around us is part of our magical practice, and universally accessible.

In fact, I would have to rely on that last statement, in order to make the case before my own ancestors and relatives, who expressed concern about my writing my two most recent books: *Magick at the Crossroads*, and this book. I proposed that if we truly embrace the truth of Essential Unity (which we'll talk about in the next section), and believe that what often gets referred to as "magic" or "what we do" (in Italian, frequently referred to as "*i vecchi modi*" — the old ways — is something that is universally accessible, then there should be no harm or detriment for me to help others, outside our family, to learn how to master those skills.

I'll share the anecdotal approach I took even further, because it's a little bit funny.

Two of the ancestors were particularly concerned with precedent, and the fact that it's been our tradition to not speak of what we do publicly, nor to ever teach someone who is outside the family, unless they've married into the family and can be trusted. And after letting them know that I too had to seriously consider this for many years, I shared that cooking was where I found the answer I needed.

"When we cook, we do so knowing that few cultures outside of Sicily and the Southern Kingdom create dishes that can compare to the rich and flavourful foods we make on a daily basis. Right?" I began.

They naturally agreed.

"And when someone marries an Americana, like my dad did, what do we do? We start with the essentials... the basics... and we slowly teach the new member of our family how to cook. It's really no different than the way we teach children how to cook, within the family. But we can move at a slightly faster pace."

The ancestors got it, and albeit a little slower to agree, so did the living relatives. I made assurances that there would be some of the things that are literally, and with good reason, "secrets" of our family's work, which would remain as such. Our history and connection to the Great Mysteries, and entheogenic "formulas" in Montecorvino Rovella, in Pompeii, and in Poggioreale, would never be something I wrote explicitly about; nor would those formulas and elixirs be something that would be appropriate for inclusion in a book like this one.

But practical magic? I can think of no other time in my own history, these past fifty-nine years on the planet, when the world hasn't desperately needed what we've so often taken for granted. And because I have literally sworn vows to do whatever I can to alleviate suffering in this world, wherever I encounter it, I cannot begin to pretend that writing this book feels more like a sacred obligation than it does "another writing project".

That was the very reason I created the Inner Alchemy Mystery School. It was our tradition that we didn't begin teaching our ways until we were fifty, and like anyone else in our family, that began with teaching the younger family members. But I also knew that there were dozens of Sicilian and Italian friends whose families didn't preserve their traditions, who were hungry for a way to reconnect with those practices.

They were not finding what they sought in pop-culture witchcraft. They were not interested in the 20th-century re-imagining and reconstruction of an old religion (or religions), because they knew such things had nothing to do with the workings they saw their grandmothers and great grandmothers doing.

And in 2016, I started with two Sicilian friends, and a couple videos on a private social media channel, which grew into twenty Italian and Sicilian friends in 2019. And in 2020, we started to allow a couple "Italian-adjacent" friends in, and the school itself, which had previously served a function only in our esoteric Franciscan community's training and formation program, officially became "Inner Alchemy Mystery School" (*La Scuola di Alchimia Interiore e gli Antichi Misteri*).

As we dive into this next section of the book, I am going to strive to cover some of those very basic and essential components of our worldview that might not be something the reader has considered before. For some, these next couple sections might cause your 'spidey senses' to tingle a bit, as it awakens parts of your DNA, perhaps even rekindling old memories, if you happen to have been born into a family of esoteric or folk magic practitioners.

These are the things I learned as a child, but I intend to present them in a more mature fashion, because this part of the project required that I read (and at times, *decipher*) notebooks and letters that I wrote as a child of seven or eight, which was as frustrating at times to figure out as it was hysterical (and embarrassing) when I would come across something I *clearly* misunderstood!

One final laugh at my expense as an example, to close out this section...

For those who don't know me personally, I was born neurodivergent — considered to be "high-functioning autistic" — a term I have come to intensely dislike. This atypical wiring of my brain often makes it a challenge, especially when I was younger, to understand that people don't literally mean what they say frequently.

There was a common expression among the aunts, uncles and my grandmother — most of whom were not born in the United States. They would say, *"Ci sono due tipi di persone nel mondo: quelli che sono italiani e quelli che vorrebbero essere italiani."* (There are two types of people in the world: those who are Italian, and those who wish they were.)

My first question when I started to understand our ways, and why we don't ever discuss them with *"Americani"* was, "Well then, why don't we turn them all into Italians, so they will be happier?!?"

So, I remember doing a bit of Catholic Conjure work, asking St. Jude to be an ally and help turn all of those who wish they were

Italian into Italians while they slept, when I was probably 7. I even found an old holy card, with his image on it, and little Sicilian flag stickers all around it, which caused me to giggle my ass off, as that memory came back to me.

But no worries... there are no spells in this grimoire that will turn you into an Italian or Sicilian! And I've tried to tease out the less mature interpretations, unless they were hysterical and needed to be included for comic relief!

Now let's get started!

Elements, Elementals & the Lase

Within the cosmology of the Afro-Sicilian and Italian magical practice are four "families" of spirits — each governed by one of the four cardinal directions, and characterised by one of the four classical elements (air, fire, water, and earth).

Together, these spirits are known as the *lase (pronounced "lah-seh")* and can best be understood to be elemental spirits.

Governed by the north, and characterised by the earth element, are the *Pale spirits (pronounced "pah-leh")*. These elementals include the *monachetti* (gnomes), the *faune* (animal spirits), the *flore* (plant spirits) and the *silvani* (tree spirits and fae).

Governed by the south, and characterised by the element of fire, are the most primal of the elemental spirits, the *settiani*; which include the *draghi* (dragons), the *djinnu* (genies), the *demoni* (daemons, angels, demons) and the *salamandre* (salamander spirits).

The *bellarie (pronounced bel-ah-ree-eh)* or sylphs are governed by the east, and represent the element of air. Among these elementals are the dream-weaver elves *(linchetti),* the spirits of the wind *(folletti),* the house faeries *(fate),* and the mischievous *monacciello* - a little monk-like trickster spirit. These elemental spirits are believed to carry out the impulse mischief of the more powerful *settiani* (fire spirits).

And finally, governed by the west, and representative of the element of water are the powerful *manii*, which include water nymphs, the undines, and the Mothers of the Waters.

Each of these groups of spirits can be powerful allies in our magical working, and have good cause for wanting to cultivate relationships with us, and cooperate with us, when we treat them with respect.

The reason for this is that elementals can only organically know the world to which they belong. In other words, the *bellarie* are adept at using the energy of the air, but know little about the element of water or fire, or earth, unless they learn from experience with multi-elemental beings, like human beings. And they have even greater impetus to want to cooperate with us, since we carry with us the knowledge of working with the Supreme Elements — *Aether and Consciousness.*

This makes for a cordial relationship, when we properly approach them. Like any relationship, we forge our relationships with these elementals from an awareness that we are essentially One. Our bodies, souls and minds are made of the very elements themselves, and are comprised, at the most foundational level, of zeropoint energy, or Source.

As a result, while the elementals can learn of the other elements through cooperating with us, we can learn to master the elements within us the more we work with the elemental spirits, in a mindful manner.

Incorporating the elements into our magical practice, and learning to work with the elemental personalities, strengths and insights can help enhance our outcomes, and deepen our connection to Source in everything we do.

The four elements in classical magical practice are Earth, Air, Fire and Water. These elements represent the fundamental aspects of reality for many people around the world. In this sense, they are not just associated with Italian and Afro-Sicilian folk magic, but also with many other religions and spiritual practices.

The four elements have been used to explain phenomena and give meaning to life since ancient times. They have also been a key component of magic throughout history. The idea is that each element has a different influence on our lives according to its nature: Earth is stable and solid, Air is light and changeable, Fire is dynamic and passionate while Water is fluid and receptive.

Throughout this text, we will frequently talk about elemental correspondences, and in certain cases, will call upon an elemental as an ally with whom we specifically work in a particular ritual or working.

Centre of the Practice, Centre of the Home

Unlike the neo-pagan traditions of the mid-20th century, in the Common Era, which is based on a religious tradition into which magical practice (and often Freemasonry) have been integrated, the magical practice of the Afro-Sicilian and Southern Italian esotericists has no connection to religion.

Therefore, it's easy to understand that our centre of practice is not a religious place, nor is it a place where groups gather for ritual activity. Those things were part of our ancestors' lives in the pre-Christian era, but they were not related to their magical practice. They were regional religious traditions, worshiping the various local gods and goddesses of the towns and provinces.

For us, the centre of practice is also the centre of our homes — the hearth or kitchen. And the place on which the vast majority of working takes place would have been the kitchen table in times past, which today may either be the kitchen table or a working counter top, butcher's block island, or something of the like. Our ancestors didn't have kitchen counters, so for them, it was the table, and for me, admittedly, I choose nostalgically to honour that tradition as well.

Our ancestors understood that real magic occurs when we are in alignment with the world around us — the planets and moon, the sun and flora, the fauna and people with whom we live and interact. They also understood that our bodies were the most powerful conduits of the Primal Energy from which all magic derives.

So, whether we are working to heal a condition, or bring about change in a relationship or financial situation… Whether we're sewing or knitting, or cooking, or cleaning… we're always doing subtle magic, because that Source Energy flows through us.

There was a wonderful illustration of these beliefs that I never quite understood, because I was assigned male at birth, and as such, would not know anything much of the reproductive cycles of those who were assigned female at birth. This would be something the aunts and grandmothers and female cousins discussed in hushed tones, and which I never thought to question or probe.

Then I had the great fortune of reading a book, written by one of my greatest Italian folk magic crushes, a nurse and practitioner living in Canada, whose name is Mary-Grace Fahrun. She wrote a book, some years ago entitled, "Italian Folk Magic[2]," and I picked up a copy in 2020, while recovering from COVID-19.

In the book, Mary-Grace talks about collecting recipes from her relatives, and recounts one time, when an aunt gave her a recipe for a particularly delicate Italian dish.

She writes:

> What was really interesting were the conversations that would evolve around the recipes. For example, one of my aunts, who was an amazing cook, warned: "But don't make this when you are on your period; it won't turn out." "But why?" I would ask. "Because there is too much power in your hands; it will ruin this delicate dish. During that time of the month, make *brodo* (broth) or braise tough meats. The power in your hands will toughen a tender filet, but will tenderize the toughest meats." Her voice dropped

---

[2] Italian Folk Magic: Rue's Kitchen Witchery, by Mary-Grace Fahrun, Weiser Books, 2018. (https://amzn.to/385O0dC)

to a whisper: "Your other aunt is in menopause. That's why her *braciole* is so tough."

Notice that the aunt spoke of the amount of power in her hands. We know that our ancestors understood the correlations between and profound connection we have to the tides, the moon, and the earth, and there is no doubt that just as the cycles of the moon affect the tides (within and without ourselves), there is a similar ecology going on with a woman's menstrual cycles. And the belief of our tradition has always been that in addition to this approach, described in Mary-Grace's book, we also be mindful of the power flowing through us at all times, before we begin to cook.

We never cook when we are angry. We especially don't cook when we are harbouring hostility toward someone who will be eating the food we make. Why? Because we're constantly circulating the power (magic) through our movements and thoughts. Food cooked by an angry cook is unhealthy, and could even be poisonous.

There is a story in our family that is somewhat amusing. When my paternal grandmother, whose family are Napolitana and Tsingare (Romani), but who was born in a small Romani enclave, south of Paris, was to meet my grandfather's family for the first time, she was nervous.

They were, by that time, particularly well known as Catholic Conjure workers, and my grandmother's people were secular practitioners of the Older Ways. And my grandmother wanted to make a good impression, so she made a fresh batch of *bombaloni* (Italian filled donuts), careful to impart great love and respect in the process, and even beginning to make them at a specific time of day, so they would be light and delicious.

Now, she also had several brothers, who were younger than her, and like most young men, were in a state of perpetually ravenous hunger. So, she hid the finished plate of *bombaloni* in her cedar chest, where the boys would not find them.

Two hours later, when the family arrived for coffee, she took out the donuts and served them, and everyone took a bite and began coughing and gagging. Turns out that putting *bombaloni* in a cedar chest results in them absorbing the cedar flavour!

Everyone had a laugh about it, because not only did they understand that there was love and a desire to win their approval behind the oversight, but as the matriarch, my Zia Maria (or Mimi, as we called her) would note, *"Almeno era una cassa di cedro, quindi ci hai benedetto con una lunga vita. Benvenuto in famiglia. Staremo qui per un po'."* ("At least it was a cedar chest, so you blessed us with a long life. Welcome to the family. We will be here for a while.")

Cedar, being the wood that coffins are made from, is believed to hold a correspondence with long life, and protection against death and decay. So, they light-heartedly teased my grandmother, and perhaps not coincidentally, everyone who took a bite of those *bombaloni,* lived well into their golden years of life. (In fact, the only two people at the table that day who didn't bite into theirs, which included my grandfather and one of his sisters, happened to die prematurely and suddenly.)

The kitchen table is where we gather as family, as friends, and as neighbours, and so it would be at the kitchen table that practitioners removed the *malocchio,* diagnosed whether a woman was pregnant, and doused to see whether it was a boy or a girl, consulted the *Scopa* cards, and of course, shared many a cup of black coffee and sweets.

When there was a death in the family, we gathered at the kitchen table, consoling one another and making whatever plans needed to be made. Remember, in my day, there was one phone in the house, and it was mounted to the wall in the kitchen, next to the table. So, it was literally a communications hub with those living and those on the other side of the veil.

Above the kitchen table, on the wall, were photos of family members no longer with us on this plane. And it was our custom to make sure there were some fresh flowers, a bowl with some fruit, and other items that might appear to simply be placed on the table, like a candle, for example, which were part of our morning ritual of sitting with the ancestors, before starting our day.

These are customs I keep to this day.

And this is also why it's rare to find a Sicilian or Italian practitioner, whose kitchen is in disarray. When the kitchen is a mess, so is your life, according to our tradition. When the energy in a kitchen is stagnant, because we've been sick, or away for a time, the first thing we do is to clean the kitchen, open the windows and doors, and clean the rest of the house.

When properly maintained, the kitchen truly is a magical world. Neo-pagan traditions frequently call for casting a circle, placing representations of the elements, calling the quarters, setting up the altar, and so forth, all before their ritual work can begin. And when my neo-pagan friends visit, they're kind of astounded that we do none of those things in our tradition.

Why?

Because the kitchen is already sacred space, and maintained as sacred space. We welcome the ancestors, and acknowledge the house spirits (*lare*) each morning. As for the elements, they're always present in the Sicilian or Italian kitchem (and probably in yours, even if you're not Sicilian or Italian):

The refrigerator and range-hood circulate AIR. Ceiling fans or windows also serve that purpose.

Cast-iron pans, wooden spoons, cutting boards, and pots of herbs are the literal elements of EARTH.

The faucet and cooler contain WATER.

And of course, the stove and oven are the source of FIRE.

You can see, for us, the centre of practice is the centre of the house, and of family life itself. The kitchen.

I would highly recommend Mary-Grace Fahrun's book, for a more in-depth look at the world of kitchen magic, because I believe it's the perfect accompaniment to this work.

The Well-Stocked Cabinet

One of the things that Mary-Grace Fahrun writes in her book that I absolutely loved is that the more spirits we welcome into our home as allies, the more powerful the space. And this is easily done by starting off your practice with a well-stocked pantry of herbs and spices.

The use of herbs and spices in magic is a very common practice.

Magic practitioners often use herbs and spices for their magical purposes. They are used for a variety of reasons, such as to make potions, to create incenses or just as decoration. There are many different types of herbs that can be used for magical purposes. Some examples include basil, lavender, sage, rosemary and peppermint.

With each plant, we begin by simply welcoming it to our home and to our kitchen. Ideally, this is done by making sure that our pantries are clean, organised and are reserved for the plants, herbs and spices alone. But if you are pressed for space, at least keep an entire shelf reserved for these plant allies.

Working with a plant ally such as an herb, root or tree has the potential to be a personal healing journey. You can also use it to gain insights into plants, herbs and other aspects of the natural world.

Relationships with plant allies takes time.

Like in human relationships, the more time and energy we put into a relationship with someone or something, the better we know them. Getting to know a plant is the same. As you get to know someone or a plant, you understand them better. As your relationship develops, so will your understanding and knowledge.

We should mention that just like people, each plant has its own set of individual qualities and personality. Some are upfront and vocal, but others will hold back until they trust you. Your relationship will be as individual as the relationship between any two beings.

When working with plant allies it is good to partner up with one that chooses you, that wants to work with you. It may not be your favourite plant, but you can trust that it will be just what you need.

This can be accomplished by taking a walk through a garden centre, in the herb section, or even walking the corridors of a farmer's market, in their plants and spices section. You'll instinctively feel drawn, when a plant is reaching out to you.

Naturally, you'll want to have the "basics" on hand, so that you can get off to a simple start. My experience has been that some of the easiest herbs and spices to work with magically are the ones we use the most often in our personal cooking or as teas.

For me, that includes basilico, bay leaf, bergamot, black pepper, blue lotus, chamomile, chili peppers, cinnamon, cumin, dandelion, garlic, lavender, marjoram, mint, mugwort, oregano, rosemary, rue, sage, spikenard, thyme, white pepper, and wormwood.

In addition to these herbs, my personal collection includes herbs and other plant materia that are not necessarily used for ingestion, including some essential oils, amanita muscaria, pennyroyal, and other ingredients that might be used in other ways in a magical working.

As you deepen your connection with this ally, it will be an ally for life. All healthy relationships with plants are a step toward healing the sense of disconnection we have with the natural world.

Afro-Sicilian Cooking - A Magical Rhythm

There is a distinctive rhythm to the way we cook and what we cook, even when we cook it, in the Afro-Sicilian and Southern Italian tradition. And that's because there is magic in everything we do, and mindfulness in each step of the process.

Now, I don't want to make it seem that the following description of foods and days of the week are written in stone, because frankly, in every region I've researched, outside of my own family's region, the specific foods on specific days are different. But curiously, one of the things that often remains the same is the "why".

So, feel free to follow your family tradition, or create one that resonates with you. The key is to decide that cooking and eating will become magical practices in and of themselves, and to establish a rhythm and predictable pattern to what you eat on which days, and why. Do this for 90-days, and see for yourself. It's one of the simplest things we do, but one of the most powerful ways to root your day-to-day life in your magical practice.

SUNDAY

Everyone knows that Sunday is the day we "make the gravy" - a time-honoured ritual that would begin before everyone else even woke up for breakfast in my home. That aroma of garlic, onion, carrot and basilico simmering in the olive oil to sweeten it just enough so that we didn't have to "ruin" it with added sugar… the meatballs frying, and sausage cooking to perfection, which would be added at just the right moment, when the tomatoes were done being sieved with an old-school tomato sieve (full disclosure, I stopped doing that years ago, because I like the seeds in my gravy)… no matter what your family called it: sugo, ragu, red sauce, or as we did "gravy", it was pure heaven.

There might even be some *bracciole*, and of course a wonderful antipasto.

And there was an anticipation around it, because Sunday was when all the family — cousins, aunts, uncles, grandparents — came together to share a feast. And that feast set the tone for another week.

MONDAY

On Monday we started the work week, and the rhythm of the Afro-Sicilian household was focused energetically on self-sustenance, good health, and abundance. So, Mondays were a day for *minestra di verdure*, which was a soup made with cannelloni beans, chard, potatoes and onions. As I grew older, it also became the night we would occasionally pair the meal with roast.

TUESDAY

On Tuesdays, it was always a chicken dish. Sometimes *piccata*, sometimes *al rosmarino,* and sometimes just roasted chicken breasts with a balsamic lime vinaigrette. It wasn't a matter of arbitrary choosing either. On Tuesday, depending on the intention, we would magically be creating a heart-warming meal that strengthened relationship (piccata), sharpened our psychic abilities and protected us from seen and unseen parasites (rosamarino), or provided us with healing protection and a sweetness of life (lime vinaigrette).

WEDNESDAY

By Wednesday, there would likely be some roast beef left over, either from Monday night, or maybe a piece or two of *bracciole* from the Sunday before. These would go into the leftover gravy from Sunday's feast and it would be another delicious pasta dinner.

The idea was that in our magic and in our lives, we leave nothing for waste. It's about ensuring that food is eaten, not tossed in the freezer and forgotten.

THURSDAY

In our home, Thursday was the day my dad would go to the butcher, and deli on the way home, because it was payday. On Saturdays, he would take us with him to the grocery store for all of the staple goods, but we loved Thursdays, because it meant he would come home with whisper-thin sliced Genoa salami, capicola, provolone and chipped ham. He'd pick up a couple loaves of "Italian bread" (crusty hoagie-type rolls) and "the good mustard". We'd have sandwiches (*sanguiche* my grandmother would call them) drizzled with garlic-infused olive oil, and topped with a little *broccoli rabe,* maybe a thin slice of onion and tomatoes, oregano, and salt and pepper.

It was a night that we celebrated the ability and blessing of a steady income, and our ability to get fresh cold cuts and cheese. Now I know that probably doesn't sound like anything special today, but growing up, there were a couple times when my dad was laid-off work for six to ten weeks, when we couldn't do that, so for us, it was an especially mindful time to be grateful for what we have.

FRIDAY

Fridays marked the end of the work week, and were a time for community celebrations. And while most Italian and Sicilian homes had fish, our house was a little different on Fridays, because my father and I were allergic to seafood.

So, Friday nights were *la frittata* night! Again, using the vegetables and herbs that were left over in the fridge, before Saturday's grocery shopping, and some delicious, fresh provolone, we'd eat with various friends, family or neighbours stopping by, maybe for a game of cards, or just to sit and chat.

This was the time that block parties would begin, and often times, preparation for special feast days that weekend would begin.

SATURDAY

My favourite day, beside Sundays was definitely Saturday, because it was when we'd wake up to the smell of fresh *brodo gallina vecchia* (old hen broth) and homemade pizza dough rising under towel-covered Pyrex bowls!

In our family, there was a *brodo* for every ailment, most of them being chicken based. And none of them were any less delicious than the next. Sometimes there might be some tortellini to go with them, sometimes it was a warm crust of leftover bread from Thursday and just the broth, with a little chopped tomatoes and onion.

My friend Mary-Grace talks about how her family did pizza dough divination regularly on Saturdays, but for my family, this was something only my grandmother's people did. The other side of the family would sit and "play *Scopa*" — a Southern Italian card game, which was actually more often used, as was the case with my family, after a hand or two, as a divination method.

So, the week would begin with a celebration of family, and end with a celebration of our ways to heal and gain insight, refining our gifts of divination and healing.

I can't imagine living my life today without that rhythm.

And fourteen years after meeting the man who became my husband in 2019, even he knows what's being served that night, based on what day of the week it is. And he likes that a lot.

Other Ingredients from My Cabinet

When I don't have these items in dried form, I have them in essential oils or tinctures for use in workings. It's important, however, that you not get bogged down with having every one of them.

It's always better to work with a handful of plant allies with whom you have cultivated a relationship, especially if they grow locally, than to get obsessed with having to have it all.

• AGRIMONY -- Harmony, Healing, Breaking Hexes, Dream Work, Protection

• ALFALFA – Good Fortune, Money Magick, Healing & Cleansing Infusions

• ALLSPICE-- Business, Luck, Success, Kindness, Money

• ANGELICA -- Repels Negativity, Divination, Purification, Success,

• ANISE -- Balance, Energy, Harmony, Purification, Well-Being

• ASTRAGALUS – Vital Energy, Shielding, Promotion of Health, Mental Clarity, Concentration

• BASIL -- Psychic Ability, Love (Reconciliation), Money, Messages/Omens

• BAY LEAF – Confers Wisdom, Strength, Vision

• BAYBERRY – Psychic Awareness, Dreams, Courage, Smudging

• BELLADONNA -- Imagination, Night Magick, Visions, Astral Realm

• BETONY -- Solving Problems, Security, Decreases Anxiety, Protection

• BLESSED THISTLE – Consecration, Protection, Healing, Cleansing by Fire

• BLUE SAGE – Smudging, Meditation, Relaxation, Ancestral Wisdom

• BLUE VERVAIN – Love Spells, Advancement Spells, Astral Travel, Initiation

• BURDOCK ROOT – Warding, Cleansing, Uncrossing, Reversal

• CALENDULA – Solar Ritual, Divination, Remembrance, Ancestral Work

• CARNATION -- Deep Love, Beauty, Communication, Fertility, Harmony, Emotions

• CATNIP -- Love, Luck, Psychic Ability, Spirits, Prevents Nightmares

• CHAMOMILE -- Blessings, Calming, Reduces Anger & Anxiety, Money, Luck

• CINNAMON -- Wealth, Money, Security, Luck, Desire, Attraction, Peace

• CINQUEFOIL (Five Finger Grass) – For the Five Blessings: Health, Money, Love, Power, & Wisdom

• CLOVE -- Divination, Prosperity, Psychic Ability, Success, Truth, Visions

• CLOVER -- Grounding, Luck, Marriage, Prosperity, Success, Spiritual Balance

• COMFREY – Healing Restoration, Safe travel

• CUMIN -- Fidelity, Harmony, The Home, Longevity, Love, Repels Negativity

- DAFFODIL -- Afterlife, Fairies, Love (Unrequited), Security, Spirits, Calming

- DAMIANA – Lust, Sex Magick, Psychic Abilities, Spirit Quests

- DANDELION -- Clairvoyance, Clarity, Divination, Communication, Spirits

- DATURA – Lycanthropy, Shape-shifting, Protection, Stupification, Spirit Quests, Insight

- DEVIL'S CLAW – Protection, Exorcism, Banishing Spells, Confounding Enemies

- DILL -- Defensive Magick, Breaking Hexes, Love, Lust, Sex Magick, Money

- ELDERBERRY – Crone Magick, Banishing, Faery Offerings

- EUCALYPTUS – Cleansing, Ritual Baths, Money Drawing, Message Delivery

- FENNEL -- Blessings, Repels Evil & Negative Energy (from entering the home)

- FEVERFEW -- Healing, Heartbreak, Love, Protection, Strength, Purification

- GALANGAL – Strength, Power, Victory, Hex-Breaking, Male Potency

- GARLIC --Banishing, Justice, Protection, Breaking Hexes, Release, Security

- GINGER -- Money, Pregnancy/ChildBirth, Moon Magick, Unity, Success

- GRAPE LEAVES – Abundance, Prosperity, Protection, Fertility

- HENBANE (highly poisonous) -- Astral Realm, Divination, Love (Attract)

- HIBISCUS – Love and Passion, Confidence, Independence

- HONEYSUCKLE -- Affection, Destiny, Happiness, Love, Peace, Well-Being

- IVY -- Attraction, Marriage, Love, Stability, Transformation, Fidelity, Omens

- JASMINE – Love, Dreams, Divination, Sensuality, Kindness

- JUNIPER BERRY – Fortune, Prosperity, Exposition of Truth

- LAVENDER -- Reduces Anger and Anxiety, Love, Manifestation, Luck, Rebirth

- LEMON BALM -- Business Success, Calming, Clarity, Fertility, Relationships

- LICORICE ROOT – Domination, Persuasion

- MANDRAKE (Poisonous) -- Desire, Courage, spirits, Wealth, Omens, Bind

- MARJORAM – Protection, Calming the Mind, Easing Grief

- MUGWORT -- Spirits, Psychic Ability, Astral Realm, Awareness, Psychic Energy

- MULLEIN – Protection, Illumination, Courage, Hedge-Crossing, Respiratory healing

- NETTLE -- Healing, Justice, Luck, Protection, Courage, Confidence

- NUTMEG -- Life, Luck, Love, Money, Power, Attract, Psychic Ability, Divination

- OREGANO – Cleansing, Healing

- ORRIS ROOT-- Astral, Protection, Relationships, Love, Sexual Attraction

- PATCHOULI -- Manifestation, Peace, Luck, Love (Attract), Money, Business

- PEPPER -- Motivation, Lust, Justice, Bind, Security, Strength

- PEPPERMINT -- Dream Work, Divination, Luck, Money, Visions, Healing

- ROSE -- Fertility, Family, Blessings, Love, Luck, Happiness, Beginnings

- ROSEMARY -- Psychic Ability, Psychic Protection, Inner Power, Luck, Afterlife

- RUE – Warding, Exorcism, Cleansing, Love-Drawing, Protection

- SAGE -- Clairvoyance, Cleansing, Visions, Clears Negativity, Business

- SANDALWOOD -- Focus, Concentration, Success, Luck, Moon Magick, Blessings

- ST. JOHN'S WORT -- Strength, Power, Money, Consecrate/Bless, Prosperity

- STAR ANISE -- Divination, Psychic Ability, Purification, Consecrate/ Bless

- SUNFLOWER -- Clarity, Dream Work, Solar Energy, Light, Peace, Money, Luck

- THYME -- Healing, Happiness, Increasing, Rebirth, Protection, Calming

- VERVAIN – Old World Wisdom, Healing, Second Sight

- VIOLET – Protection, Warding, Energetic Warding

• WORMWOOD -- Clairvoyance, Dream Work, Guidance, Psychic Ability, Spirits

• YARROW -- Defense, Banishing, Heartbreak, Marriage, Healing, Release, Strength

We have arranged for readers of this book to have access to an organic, ethically-sourced and fair-trade resource for nearly all of these essential oils and more, at significant savings over some of the less ethical "direct sales" and "network marketing" companies that are so popular online today.

Simply Earth earmarks 13% of profits company-wide to fight global trafficking, and offers one of the most comprehensive programs for learning to work with essential oils I've seen in years. You can get your direct discount and learn more by visiting:

https://simplyearth.com/?rfsn=3482336.ec7739

CHAPTER TWO

Ancestors, Death & Dying

"Ancestor veneration and the work that goes with it have long been a shadowed practice in much of the West, finding its deepest expression in genealogy and family stories."

H. Byron Ballard, author of Seasons of a Magical Life

Shaping My View on Death Magic

We'll start this section with an entry from my journal, in January 2004:

Today, the American Academy of Arts and Sciences finally elected the brilliant religious historian and medievalist, Professor Richard Kieckhefer into the academy.

Of course, I have been a student of his writing, and a grateful admirer of his insights and service to the Societas Magica -- an organisation dedicated to furthering communication and exchange among scholars interested in the study of magic, both in the positive contexts of its expression as an area of necessary knowledge or religious practice (as in early modern occultism and contemporary paganism), and in its negative contexts as the substance of an accusation or condemnation (as in sorcery trials, and many philosophical and theological accounts, both early and late), over which he presided for quite a number of years.

And while his research has been invaluable during my own research into the magical traditions of ancient Sicily and Southern Italy, as well as my growing interest into the pre-institutional and profoundly metaphysical roots of the proto-catholic movement as a mystery school tradition, steeped in a psychedelic sacramental experience, I have always been impressed with his classifications of magical practice (while loathing his choice of words for them).

Kieckhefer refers to two major categories of magic: "low" magic includes charms (prayers, blessings, adjurations), protective amulets and talismans, sorcery (the misuse of medical and protective magic, sometimes referred to as "poisoning" or the poison path), divination, and medical magic through herbs and animals; and "high," or intellectual, magic, includes more learned forms of astrology, astral magic, alchemy, books of secrets, and necromancy. I found his classifications to be useful, because they show us how little the world outside of our culture actually understood the dynamics that gender constructs have played in the development of our tradition, and those traditions that grew out of it.

Traditional "male" studies would have included the intellectual paths, while the more practical, healing and grassroots studies were traditionally held by "women".

And I have to believe that this is one of those phenomena that we can find repeated in other cultures around the world.

Bishop Thomas Grady charged the members of the Contemplative Order of Compassion (then known simply as the Franciscan Companions of the Immaculata) with a mission to serve and bring compassion, love and healing of the Divine Feminine aspect of Source to those dying with AIDS, at a time when no one in his diocese would do so. And he recognised that in order for this powerful opportunity for consecrated religious (contemplatives) to bring the proto-catholic mysteries to those who were marginalised, discarded and dying alone in hospitals and hospices, would require a sub rosa return to a time when the rules and confines of dual-gender notions were set aside, as they once were in the ancient world of the mystics, and Desert Fathers/Mothers.

Bishop Grady left the mortal coil behind two years ago, and tonight I will be consecrated as a bishop at the African American

Catholic Congregation's Imani Temple and Cathedral, here in Washington, D.C., ensuring that a way forward for us, without regard for forced constructs of gender, race and orthodoxy; which can now be permanently left to the dust-heap of colonialist, institutional religion, where they belong.

This will finally allow us to deepen the work we do with those who are dying, by opening the doors to a richer and fuller experience of the entheogenic sacrament and psychedelic magical practices designed to bring those preparing to shed their mortal coil back into conscious unity with Source and their Personal Power.

It was clear to me, as I re-read that old entry, that my focus throughout my adult life, has differed considerably from so many of my contemporaries in that I understood the Afro- Sicilian and Southern Italian tradition's rootedness in working with the ancestors as not only being one of the most important aspects of our work, but literally as being the foundation of all magic itself.

Kieckhefer's classifications helped me to understand how my tradition would be viewed by outsiders, including many of those I would serve, in hospices, hospitals and their homes, in the final days and hours of their lives.

For them, this duality of "high magic" and "low magic" would inform the way in which they may have interacted with the magical world for decades, and may have represented the fundamental causes for many of the obstacles, hardships and disappointments in their spiritual journeys along the way.

If I was going to be an effective death doula, then I needed to be able to offer those I served a fresh look at the three pillars of my people's tradition -- Nature, Mind and Heart.

Natural magic was where we encounter the plant and animal allies, learning how to work with them in partnership, alliance and respect for healing, energising our work, and sustaining the world in which we live, as its stewards.

Mind magic was the intellectual, philosophical, Hermetic and Great Mystery traditions of our people and the cultures who contributed to our evolution along the way, and as such, includes science, and the study of Chaos and Quantum magic.

And Heart magic is the oldest of all magic, because it is the magic of the ancestors. Influenced by culture, blood, mythos and the traumas that our ancestors shared, we recognise that before they were on the Isle of Sicily, our African ancestors understood that the very first ancestors we honoured were our plant ancestors, Dada, in the Yoruba language.

From that Primordial Sacred Grove, which I believe science is beginning to recognise now as the fungal network beneath the surface of the forests, our first human ancestors (the Òrìsà) came.

Today, this physical body I possess represents the combined contributions of my direct ancestors. And this means for me that I must always, first and foremost, see myself as the first offering being made in gratitude back to those of which I am a representative part.

So, this chapter is a bit of a tricky one, because I have experienced that each of us really must do the work ourselves, and connect with, then cultivate relationships with our own ancestors, to understand what ancestral veneration should look like.

Within my family, there are ancestors on the Afro-Sicilian side, whose practices ranged from secular magical practice to Catholic Conjure, and on the Romanian-Hungarian side, there are both practitioners of Roma (Romani) magic, and Baltic Catholic folk-magic practices. Therefore, the ways in which I connect with those ancestors differs, depending on their culture, their beliefs and the relationships I have cultivated with them.

I have certainly cultivated a far greater number of relationships with the Afro-Sicilian and Southern Italian side of my ancestors, with only five or six relationships presently existing with the Eastern European and Romani side of the family.

So, these spells I share will mostly come from the oldest of the spells handed down to me, in order to represent the broadest application from my experience. I encourage you to allow the spells to sort of "wash over you" and see if you are inspired to adapt them, rather than simply adopting them.

Let your ancestors speak, if only in a whispered word or two, to guide you along your way, when it comes to the magic we do to honour our ancestors, and the magic specifically geared toward death and dying.

The soul's journey to the next world begins when the dying person begins showing signs of losing consciousness.

This is often a period of 24 to 72 hours before physical death occurs. It is a gradual process, a long journey, and subsequently must be attended to by the family, loved ones, and wider community.

Rituals are performed by laypeople, priests, and folk healers to assure safe passage. These may include opening a window, removing metal chains from the neck, cooling the forehead of the dying person, reciting rosaries or other prayers.

The purpose of these actions is to comfort the person who is preparing to leave this plane, by reassuring them that it's safe and that their loved ones will be alright. We speak of this in psychological terms as "giving them permission to die".

And this phase of the dying process is critical, because those who have to accomplished this sense of awareness that it's OK to die may become bound to this realm, where they remain as ghosts, until we help them sever those attachments.

Those who die suddenly, unexpectedly or violently will often retain strong ties to the living, as they were unprepared for their departure.

And so, we will often seek out the involvement of more experienced practitioners to help the ancestors caught in such traumatic loss of life to ease the transition and release the bonds that hold them captive, frequently to the place of their death.

In more normal cases, once the person has made their transition, our customs include washing the corpse, putting food and water nearby so the soul can maintain its strength, and talking to the corpse in a reassuring manner.

We have a folk belief in Catholic Conjure that the deceased will be met, either by their mother or by the Blessed Mother, who will take them across the mythical Ponte di San Giacomo -- a bridge that connects this world with the afterlife, which likely stems from ancient myth is about the Milky Way allegedly being such a bridge, created from the breast milk of the ancient Roman goddess, Juno.

One way we can personally be assured to have the strength and support of our ancestors, when a loved one is preparing to die, is to begin cultivating an ancestral practice as an essential ritual of our daily lives.

Essential Ancestral Practice

Edmund Burke wrote, in Reflections on the Revolution in France, "People will not look forward to posterity who never look backward to their ancestors."

Through the practice of illuminating the road back to our ancestors, and by the steadfast cultivation of meaningful relationships with them, we realise the enormous and almost limitless potential for creating something powerful.

The author, Raquel Cepeda put it this way, "Individually, every grain of sand brushing against my hands represents a story, an experience, and a block for me to build upon for the next generation."

Establishing an ancestral practice literally begins with cultivating a meaningful relationship with our beloved dead. There's no need to try, right off the bat, to have a relationship with your ancestors from the reign of Emperor Tiberius, when you already knew your grandma or great aunts, who crossed over.

Start off by working with them. You already know them, and will be more comfortable sitting down with them each day.

If you didn't get along with them, then consider starting off with a general petition to welcome "all the ancestors from all the realms" to sit with you, so that you can show them your appreciation.

Begin with a clean home, and an uncluttered kitchen table. On a nice, clean, pressed tea towel or placemat, set out your offerings to the ancestors. For me, it's a cup of coffee (cappuccino in the morning, espresso in the early evening) with a small plate on which I may place biscotti, a few santini (holy cards), maybe a rosary, and a tea light.

In Montecorvino, we would use rosewater (sort of a rose hydrosol) spray mist to clear the air, and welcome them in.

Then just sit. It might seem fruitless the first couple times, but I find that talking with them, and then just sitting quietly will eventually get the ball rolling.

This is the central and most important working we can do, and is something I encourage you to make time for every day.

As a teacher, I get to hear more than my share of excuses. And the greatest purveyors of excuses for not being able to "keep up" with their studies, or be as effective in their spiritual works always comes from those who have forgotten to make their ancestral practice a central, luminous and important part of their daily lives.

There will always be interruptions, kids' concerts, work meetings, or weather issues to contend with in life. None of these things are ever the reason for your lacking connection with your ancestors. There is only one reason -- all excuses are equal. Either you make it essential and a priority, or you don't. And they will respond accordingly.

They always do.

Those who have come before us are those on whose shoulders we stand in this life. So, it's fitting that we honour and respect them. In our tradition, we believe that each of us is connected through the "golden thread" that arises out of the top of our heads to one of the oldest of our ancestors. I suspect that this idea has direct ties to the beliefs of our ancestors who came to Sicily from Africa, and would later be syncretised with Folk Catholic stories of "guardian angels" or "patrons and patronesses".

In recent years, having to work with a significantly reduced amount of living space in our home, we had to dismantle the more traditional placement of the ancestral altar/table, above which our beloved ancestors' pictures would hang on the wall. Resembling a family tree, but consisting only of those who departed, the higher up on the wall you looked, were the oldest and longest departed family members.

It was not uncommon to have images of our saints and Great Ancestors at the highest level, and in our home, crowned with images of the Sacred and Immaculate Hearts.

Today, we don't have the room on the wall for those images, and so a smaller table has group photos of some of the more recently departed family members, and emblematic pieces, such as an old skull, keys, books and other items that represent the combined communion of our Beloved Departed.

We set out three or six bowls of water, some flowers, when possible, and fresh daily incense every morning, and bow to them each night before turning in for the night.

You need not enslave yourself to doing more than is possible. A small corner of your table, with a placemat and photo of one or two particular loved ones, a flower and bowl of water may be enough.

Do I really believe that the ancestors are watching over us?

It's not a question of belief, and I am disinclined to recommend that anyone simply "believe" or "disbelieve" in such things. This is something you can actively experiment with and determine through your lived experience, if it is as worth it for you as it has been for the past five decades of my life, serving at the discretion of my Sacred Ancestors of time, of blood, of tribe and culture.

Ritual Death Work

It's been said that death is a foreign land, and that one day, we will all find ourselves as immigrants there. This is one of the reasons we work so closely with our ancestors, because they can become our most important teachers when it comes to understanding not only how to ease the transition of those we love, but how to prepare ourselves for that day in our own journeys.

When death approaches for someone we love, in our tradition, a white plate, with sea salt in the centre, and a white votive candle (usually in a red glass votive holder) is placed in the centre of the plate. The plate is decorated with springs of rue and juniper, and lavender flowers, sometimes woven into a wreath surrounding the candle. This plate may also hold a rosary belonging to someone (an ancestor) who has already crossed over, santini (holy cards) or photos of the deceased parents or grandparents, inviting them to be present to the person who is preparing for their transition from life.

Immediately Upon the Death of a Loved One

In our tradition, it remains preferable that our loved ones die at home, when possible. Hospice care makes this possible today, under better circumstances than we often faced in ages past.

When the loved one has passed, open the windows and doors. Then take the kitchen broom and sweep the entire house, including the ceiling corners, where cobwebs or spider webs might exist. The dust and debris should be buried outside, and the broom should be broken, and left at a crossroads. Someone close to you should purchase a new broom and bring it into the house, placing it with the broom upright, behind the front door.

If Unresolved Anger or Resentment Exists

In his book, *The Place We Call Home: Exploring The Soul's Existence After Death*, Robert J. Grant says:

"The free will every human being possesses in life continues after death. Only when the soul relinquishes its hold upon malice, hate, vengeance, and the things of the material world in order to embrace the light can the greater light come in.

How quickly the process of leaving behind the material thoughts and desires after death goes is very much dependent upon how much spiritual consciousness is cultivated during the life on earth."

For our part, we should always do whatever we can to ensure that any ill-will, anger or lack of forgiveness in which we play a part is either resolved before the person passes, or is accomplished at their grave site, within 24 to 48 hours of their being laid to rest.

(If a person is cremated, this can still be done, wherever that funereal urn will be placed and honoured.)

Making Peace and Healing Life's Loose Ends Spell

Approach the grave site or resting place of the deceased, and make an offering of spring water, with a few drops of Angostura™ bitters added to it.

Say, "For any of the times my words, deeds or thoughts brought bitterness to your life, I am sorry."

If they have done wrong to you, state your forgiveness for them as well to release any hold you have on that past energy.

A second bottle of spring water, in which you've poured some honey, should then be offered.

"May the way between us always be sweet, and may our souls know that love is always greater than fear and anger."

A final offering of juniper berries (or some fragrant gin) is then offered, and we sit for a few moments with the departed loved one, and send our love, saying our goodbyes, as necessary.

Gifted author, Chris Allaun writes in *A Guide of Spirits*[3]:

Ascended ancestors make wonderful Psychopomp Teachers because they know what it is like to be human. They once had human weaknesses, fears, and many other faults that make us human. They can teach us many things in our psychopomp work which include having compassion for the people we are working with. The ascended ancestors also have a deeper understanding

---

[3]   A Guide of Spirits, Chris Allaun (Moon Books) 2021 - https://amzn.to/3tM7paW

for the work that we are doing and can teach us to have patience with ourselves.

The pop-culture, neo-pagan world suffers no shortage of spell books and magical formularies. From classics, written in the mid-twentieth century, by some of the founders and creators of the neo-pagan magical traditions, such as Wicca, Alexandrian Witchcraft, Gardnerian Witchcraft and British Traditional Craft, to the more modern traditions of the 80s and 90s, a wealth of material has been written.

Seeing promise in the growing number of attempts to blend a re-imagined combination of occult and esoteric practices (largely derived from the accusations made by the Roman Catholic and Anglican churches, in the 15th through the 18th centuries, against herbalists, folk magic practitioners, midwives and psychics, whom they deemed to be "witches") with a revival of ancient polytheistic religious cults (particularly of Roman, Etruscan and Greek origin), once small publishers of astrological booklets and farming almanacs evolved into multi-million dollar annual revenue producers.

And despite the problematic backstories and pretentious claims that many of those neo-pagan religious sects of the mid-twentieth century ought to have been plagued by, the movement took off. With influences that were connected to 19th-century Romanticism, and often extremist views of the nationalist and fascist founders of some of these traditions, somehow people would choose to ignore these problems, and focus instead on the promise of reviving something that seldom bears even a remote resemblance to the ancient religious sects of antiquity.

The result has been an abundance of "how-to" books on everything from common household spells and charms, to more elaborate ritual magic and claims to recreate the sigil magic of King Solomon. Some of those texts have become among the most highly respected works in the neo-pagan canon, including the works of Scott Cunningham, Sybil Leek, Alex Sanders, Doreen Valiente, and Raymond Buckland.

Modern practitioners of the neo-pagan and pop-culture witchcraft traditions include what I would consider to be an even more brilliant and respectable assembly of authors, including Judika Illes, Mat Auryn, Chris Allaun, Laura Tempest Zakroff, Devin Hunter, Storm Faerywolf, Denise Alvarez, Chas Bogan, Michael Hearkes, and Skye Alexander. These incredible and visionary teachers, practitioners, artists and writers have made a considerable mark on the neo-pagan witchcraft community that has elevated it beyond anything the respected elders of years gone by could have imagined possible.

This book does not seek to be like anything those remarkable authors and practitioners have ever produced. Their work stands on its own, and serves the neo-pagan and pop-culture witchcraft community in ways that are authentic, rich and praiseworthy.

This book, *Songs of the Night Skies: A Grimoire of Healing, Transformation and Justice*, was written for an entirely different, and often seemingly invisible audience. Neither born out of the neo-pagan religious approach to witchcraft, nor focused on any of the derivative pop-culture approaches of the 80s, 90s and aughts, this book is the accumulation of a little more than a half-century of authentic, gritty, unglamourous esoteric and magical practice, by an hereditary practitioner of the ancient Afro-Sicilian and Southern Italian folk magic traditions.

It's derived from hundreds of journals, cookbooks, letters and lived experiences that I've accumulated over the years, since my "initiation" at the age of six, when I learned on Christmas Eve, how to diagnose and remove il malocchio (the evil eye), up until the present day.

Much as the Afro-Sicilian and Southern Italian magical tradition doesn't remotely resemble what one calls to mind when the word "witchcraft" is mentioned, this grimoire likely won't easily resemble what comes to mind when most readers think of the word "grimoire" either. And that's because, despite the fanciful but baseless claims that Gerald Gardner's tradition hearkens back to an imaginary magical tradition in the wooded groves of Tuscany, there is no neo-pagan equivalent to the actual and authentic magical practices of the ancient Italian and Afro-Sicilian worlds.

Will there be spells found in these pages? Absolutely. Is there magical instruction for dealing with many of the most common concerns we face in the postmodern world? Without question.

Grimoires are defined as books of instructions in the use of magic, alchemy and metaphysics; and without doubt, the reader will find in these pages plentiful instruction, once-hidden knowledge, and insight into the ways in which my ancestors have practiced magic and esotericism for the past 3,000 years, if the oral tradition is to be believed.

But this book is also written by an anthropologist, an historian, and a pragmatist. So, it will also be a more practical guide than some of the spell books and grimoires that are in publication, because I've attempted to weave into the ancient practices that I will share with you some postmodern insight, including scientific understanding, which can be seen as validation that our ancestors "were onto something", and science just hadn't fully caught up yet. In many cases, science still hasn't caught up. And so there will be some spells that "just work", for which I can offer neither an explanation nor further insight.

I've chosen only to include the spells, charms, rituals and formulas that I've personally used, so that I could offer whatever practical insight might arise from that experience.

Legally, I am bound to remind the reader that this book is intended to be read as an anecdotal reference only, since many of the ingredients used in some of the workings described in this volume are potentially poisonous or deadly. So consider these pages to be offered as anecdotes and historical context materials, copied from the real-life journals and notebooks of a spiritual practitioner, mystagogue, esotericist, herbalist, and what my people would simply call, a "*fattucchiero*" or magical worker, and a "*guaritore*" or healer.

Science is discovering new ways in which many of these old formulas can truly be transformative and healing every day.

We need look no further for evidence of this than to consider the use of entheogenic substances, like *amanita muscaria* (magic mushrooms). Entheogenic medicine has been part of the Afro-Sicilian and Italian esoteric traditions for millennia. Long understood for their ability to restore mental homeostasis at lower doses, it was also the foundation of sacred medicines that allow us to connect more deeply with the ancestors and Source on a fourth dimensional level, often understood as existing outside of the three-dimensional constructs of time and space.

In recent years, science has studied and validated the positive impact this sacred medicine can have on people suffering from mental health issues, as well as those struggling with life-threatening dis-ease.

It's use as a sacrament in the Mystery Traditions, including (as many now suspect) the possibility of it being at the foundation of the pre-institutional Christian mysteries, is recognised as the "magical bridge" between the mundane and ethereal levels of consciousness.

So you know the drill… "Neither the author nor the publisher accepts any liability for how the reader chooses to use this information. Use at your own discretion and risk."

Blah-blah-blah.

Just use this information responsibly, ethically, and be blessed. If it helps inspire you to live your best life, I will have accomplished everything I set out to accomplish, when I began compiling the various spells and workings into this grimoire at the start of the COVID-19 pandemic, while recovering from COVID myself.

I think it's also important to understand another way in which this grimoire might be a bit different from what is commonly found on bookshelves in the pop-culture esoteric and occult worlds.

This volume is not intended to simply be a spellbook or catalogue of recipes. I think perhaps, if you will indulge me, this book could best be viewed as a living instructional essence — a liminal bridge that has the potential to connect with your innate wisdom in such a way that it unlocks deeper mysteries than you will find in the mere words and formularies contained on the printed pages.

I've been told by the people who have worked with the rough draft texts of this book over the past ten years that it's something that completely changes for them every couple years. Almost like it becomes a new book, as their wisdom, compassion and insight deepens.

And so that tells me that it's not the text or the author that's changing things, but the magic itself, which is wholly indwelling.

I think that there are plenty of wonderful books that offer the everyday "how-to" spells for love and relationships, money and career, health and home, etc. This book was written from my personal experiences... literally transposed from notebooks and journals, sheets of paper tucked away in other books... and I've selected the workings that I believe have the greatest potential to heal, transform, awaken and empower the reader.

Again, while the information and instruction in this book can work for anyone, it's important to understand that this book is not written from a neo-pagan or theistic perspective in any way. You may wish to adapt the information to work within theistic constructs and mythologies, if that's something that is central to your magical working.

Religion plays no role at all in my tradition, and while there were some early entries in my notebooks that explored whether or not I should incorporate religion into my practice, the way my neo-pagan friends did, I've chosen to leave that material out of the book, so as to avoid confusing the focus and intention of this work.

This book's usefulness will largely be dependent upon the reader. As a teacher, I get to hear more than my share of excuses. And the greatest purveyors of excuses for not being able to "keep up" with their studies, or be as effective in their spiritual works always comes from those who have forgotten to make their ancestral practice a central, luminous and important part of their daily lives.

There will always be interruptions, kids' concerts, work meetings, or weather issues to contend with in life. None of these things are ever the reason for your lacking connection with your ancestors. There is only one reason -- all excuses are equal. Either you make it essential and a priority, or you don't. And they will respond accordingly.

They always do.

And our ancestral practice is central to our way of moving and working our magic in this world.

Thank you for deciding to pick the book up. The book itself is a spell, intended to only be opened by those who would benefit from it in some way. So I hope you will take time to share with me and with others what your thoughts are after reading it and using it in your practice.

CHAPTER THREE

The Way of the Strega

Our Way of Being in the World

"You don't look like a witch," was always one of those phrases that drove me nuts as a young person. I mean, honestly, I was struggling enough as it was with my gender identity, my cultural identity, and all things queer about me, and did not need to try to figure out if I would ever "fit in" with the societal construct of what a modern with was or was not.

Of course, at other times, given my affinity for black nail lacquer, and a tendency to mostly where black shirts and genes, with an occasional flair for naturally shadowy eyes (with or without cosmetic assistance), people would tell me, "Oh, I clocked you as a witch the first time I saw you."

Throughout my life, however, there was one constant…

I was a queer person, whose magical practice was not like the majority of those I had come to know in the pop-culture "witch" scene. And so, I didn't really identify with them. I wasn't neo-pagan, I already performed in drag, so I had little interest in incorporating "dress up" in my magical practice, and because our culture didn't identify with the notion of being "witches" or "strega", I held in contempt the 20th century pop-culture icons, especially those who were peddling a distorted, culturally inaccurate and irrelevant Wiccan-themed traditions, with Italian appropriations attached to them (or as my aunt would say, "Wicca with Italian herbs and seasonings is still Wicca… it's nothing like our ancestors' ways.")

My Zio Leo (Dr. Leo Martello) intended to create a 20th century adaptation of Wicca, with a crossover tie to his impressions of the *Vecchia Religione*, and he called it the "Way of the Strega". This of course, was done tongue-in-cheek, and with a wink-wink, nod-nod to the lies and fanciful backstories being peddled by many of his contemporaries in the pop-culture witchcraft world. He also knew that some less scrupulous individuals would attempt to plagiarise his work, and by never (with the exception of one interview with Margot Atwood) discussing his own made-up backstory, he set the perfect trap for these 20th century hucksters to make laughing stocks of themselves outside of Salem's and New Orleans' most gullible consumers.

"No actual Italian or Sicilian would ever consider the bullshit that these con-artists are writing books about today as *'stregheria'* to be serious. We know better. The way of the *'strega'* has always been the way of everyday life, and the blood, sweat and tears our people suffered under the authoritarian church, the empire that attempted to homogenise us, our language and our cultures, and the intolerance we experienced in the New World," he once told us at Sunday dinner. So when they steal my words, they will make mockeries of themselves, and expose themselves as the vermin they have always been.

My experience has been that he was spot-on right. The figures in Salem, Pittsburgh, New Orleans and elsewhere who attempted to profiteer from Zio Leo's work have all, one-by-one been exposed as frauds.

My Honesty at Great Personal Cost

I've been unapologetic in my criticism of people like the late neo-pagan (Wiccan) author, Raven Grimassi, whose grotesque misrepresentation of the Italian and Sicilian magical practices are responsible for much of the misinformation being circulated in the Americas about the subject.

I make no personal judgment of his character, as I find such things irrelevant to my own work, and to my ancestral tradition.

In his later years, I had the opportunity to speak with him, at considerable length, on two occasions, and made no bones about the issues I had with what he purported in his books. And I found him to be remarkably affable and honest about his unfortunate choices made early-on in his writing career.

But my criticism has not been without cost.

Many of the authors, teachers and practitioners, particularly those associated with publishing companies that have developed a reputation for cultural appropriation, have happily made themselves available on my podcast platform to promote their work, while refusing to even read any of my work, out of fear that they might have to deconstruct the mythologies they've created around characters like Grimassi, Bruno, Day, *et al.*

But Grimassi himself admits:

My first attempts at providing information on the Italian Craft began around 1979 with the self publication of books and a magazine. Working from material I had copied in my late teens and early twenties, I created an "outer-court" system through which I could convey the basic concepts of initiate teachings. Looking back on these early projects they were crude and amateurish. But for the time period they seemed to fit in with what most people were producing. ...Thinking back on those days now I realize that I was a "true believer" in the things I had been taught and had learned. I think this was no more evident than in my writings on Aradia, which I presented in a self published work titled The Book of the Holy Strega.

Grimassi's fabricated tradition drew heavily on surmised Etruscan mythology, which not only has nothing to do with the cultures of Sicily and the *Mezzogiorno* region of Southern Italy, but is entirely about religion, and not the practice of Italian folk-magic in any way.

In the absence of forging a deep relationship with the cultures from which these practices come, it's difficult at best to truly appreciate them; and if practiced without that proper respect and context, it's simply cultural appropriation, which is precisely how I categorise the *Wicca-with-Oregano* traditions of Grimassi, Bruno and their cults.

So, what is the way of the Strega?

In recent years, partially because of pop-culture publishing companies, and YouTube channels, the word strega has become less and less of a pejorative term (in English speaking countries), because many people began to reclaim it for themselves.

Unfortunately, most of those who reclaimed it were using it in the Wiccan sense of the word, and their practices don't remotely resemble the actual ways of our ancestors; and in Italian-speaking countries, the word still carries with it the disdain and scorn that has always accompanied calling someone strega.

The truth is that *strega* is simply the word for "witch" in many Italian dialects and languages. And for about a decade. I reclaimed the word as well. And I unapologetically use the term from time to time, when describing what we are.

But there really is a problem with the idea of calling practitioners of Italian and Afro-Sicilian magic "*streghe*[4]".

In order to unpack the problem with the word, we can first lightly acknowledge that no one in the ancient world called themselves witches. That was a term used by the authorities (which usually meant by the Roman Catholic Church and Roman Empire) to cast aspersion on those perceived as representing a threat to their authority. Many times, these were the midwives, the herbalists, the cartomancers, the story-tellers, the wise women and wise men, and the revolutionaries.

And in that realisation, we can partially unpack the problems with the term.

For us, there was never a single type of person who practiced "*stregoneria*" (witchcraft), principally because (and yes, I will keep driving this point home) none of us considered what we were doing to be "stregoneria". Yes, we worked our ways magically, but not as an anomaly. We understood that each of us live and move through a magical cosmos, and have access to that magic every moment of every day.

I love how Moïra Fowley-Doyle put it in her book, *Spellbook of the Lost and Found,* where she writes, "You cast spells every day. Your makeup is glamor magic. Hiding and highlighting. The clothes you pick out to make your legs look longer, your waist smaller. The red you wear for confidence; the black when you're sad, the blue for clarity. Your favorite bra. Your lucky socks. The way you take an hour on your hair. It's a ritual. It's never just about clothes, or makeup, or perfectly messy buns. It's about magic."

So, there were some people who had a way with working with the plant spirits, and herbal treatments, for when people were sick. They existed long before, and eventually inspired and would become some of the finest doctors. There were some who were

---

[4] Streghe is the plural for strega. Technically, the masculine form of strega is stregone, which I don't personally use, being genderqueer.

gifted artists, who could create images that lifted the mood, or protected our homes. These people would become known as great artists over time. Some were dedicated midwives, and others worked as animal whisperers. There were those who could see into the future, and others who could communicate with those who had left this plane of existence.

It's essential to remember that Italy did not exist as a unified country until 1861, and the imposition of a "national language" came much later. In fact, Italian did not become the official language of Italy until 2007 C.E.

It's also important to realise that 87% of the surviving folk magick practices known today come from the Southern Italian and Sicilian cultures. And for us, we wouldn't have (and didn't) refer to our practices as *stregoneria*.

Maybe there was that woman your grandmother didn't care for, about whom she and your cousins might gossip in hushed tones, around the kitchen table, calling her "that strega putana", but we'd never refer to our own practices as stregoneria. That was one of the most frequent arguments I recall happening between my Zia Maria, Zia Irenelle and Zio Leo.

Leo Martello was cultivating a name for himself with his "Way of the Strega" booklet, and he felt we would be more empowered by reclaiming the word — in English and in Italian — which was a popular idea in mainstream American culture in the 60s.

And so, for the purpose of this book, and because I grew up with one foot in each culture, I will alternatively refer to "our ways" as stregoneria or simply "our ways".

Our ways, *stregoneria* if you like, but often called *fattucchiera* (sorcery), *guarigione* (healing) *and fa lu santuccio* (a little holy thing) were as much a part of everyday life as anything else. It was folk magic and ancestral veneration, akin to some of the forms of folk magic we find in the Afro-American and Afro-Caribbean Disaporic traditions. It was a system not only of magic, but as we illustrated in the previous section, when talking about the foods we eat on certain days of the week, a system of moving through the world. It was a cultural expression of who we were as Afro-Sicilian and Southern Italian people.

So yes, you could say that we are conjure workers, much in the same sense that you can say that a Hoodoo practitioner is a conjure worker, but the two are only distantly related, and each deserves respect for its unique cultural expression. Surely, we are divinators, but unlike some of the more pop-cultural forms of divination, ours has subtle cultural influences that really only make sense within our culture and history.

On Cultural Appropriation

You see, I don't mind that people like Raven Grimassi and Lori Bruno created their own religious interpretations of Wicca and passed it off as "Italian Witchcraft", because I know that practitioners of Afro-Sicilian and Italian folk magic don't identify with Wicca or the pop-culture notion of "witchcraft", and we certainly don't conflate our magical practices with our religious practices. The two may overlap, just as a tablecloth overlaps the table, but doesn't *become* the table, it simply intersects with there the dishes sit upon the table.

What I do mind is when people are dishonest about such things. And I am not talking about their absurd backstories, their claims of being "initiated" by family in Sicilia, or any of that patently obvious horse shit. I mind when they claim that their Italian-themed Wicca is derived from the ways of my people... my ancestors... and the ancestors of all of those from the Kingdom of Sicily and our African ancestors. And I am particularly offended when they profiteer off such claims.

A close examination of the authentic magical practices of the Afro-Sicilian and Southern Italian culture would reveal a great deal of intersectionality with the folk magic traditions of the Tunisians, the philosophies of the Kemetic people, the traditions of the Celts and Norms, Persian mysticism and Greek wisdom. Humanity evolves outside of a vacuum. And that means we will always be influenced by what we learn from others.

I was born into our tradition, and for that I am grateful. But there are literally close to one hundred students in the Inner Alchemy Mystery School — a community of learning and social support that I created — whom I have personally invited to learn the ways of my people.

Originally, almost every one of them were Sicilian. Then we added in some wonderful folks from the Northern Italian regions, then some French, some African Americans, some Irish Canadians, and today we have students from eleven countries and representing nine nationalities. They walk the path of stregoneria by invitation, and they are as much my siblings as those born into my family of origin.

And they will never claim the tradition to be something other than what it is. They won't profiteer, or claim to have been initiated into some secretive sect, so that they can go start their own school. And because I personally find such things a bit ego-maniacal and distasteful, neither will they ever call themselves "Salvato witches", because, well, they're not Salvatos! And my ego doesn't need to be stroked or my pocket lined every time someone teaches a class, or heals a child, or helps someone communicate with a loved one who is no longer in this world.

I Do Nothing Without My Ancestors' Guidance

This book took forever for me to write it, even though it was the most requested topic at every workshop I've ever done over the past decade; and that's because the ancestors were hesitant about how we would go about sharing what we do with a world that might confuse our ways with pop-culture neo-pagan witchcraft.

But when the time came that it made sense... that our world needed a sensible approach to living a magical life that didn't rely on Greek, Persian, African, Etruscan, Roman, Celtic or Norse mythology and religious reconstruction, for those who, like me, had no interest in religion, and who felt no need to worship any deity... then they said, "So? What are you waiting for? Get to work. No more excuses! You've been busting our chops for 24 years about this, and now you know what you have to do!"

As a result, if you've read this far into this book, I have a surprise for you. And it's a personal surprise!

I've never written a book that wasn't consecrated ritually at the end of its writing, after the last of the edits were made. And unlike all of the other books, which strictly got consecrated to my ancestors, this one was consecrated to my ancestors and to the mothers and fathers of all the ancestors of those who pick up this book.

Therefore, right now, as you read this, you are being personally invited to study our practice, and if it feels like a good fit for you, to freely adopt it as part of your own unique and individual expression of magic in the world.

"We don't choose the tradition," Zia Maria would tell me, "the tradition chose us."

So if you're here, you're here for a reason, and I celebrate that with you!

"...magic is older than writing. So nobody knows how it started."

— Zora Neale Hurston

Ritual Tools of Our Tradition

Unlike Wicca, in which magical tools which both honour a deity and serve a functional purpose in the working of the magical ritual, the tools used in the Afro-Sicilian and Italian folk magic traditions are purely practical.

The main reason for this difference is that neo-pagan magical practice combines bits borrowed from Freemasonry, Rosicrucianism, 19th century occultism, Golden Dawn and literature, mythology and the imagination of Gerald Gardner. And because his symbolism and tradition has been largely accepted by modern neo-pagan adherents, and admired for the aesthetic beauty those symbols represent, they endure in the 21st century.

Similarly, in our tradition, without connections to religious worship and primitive mythology, our tools are more practical and pragmatic. As such, they endure as well. It's been said, according to our oral tradition that we chose commonplace and practical tools as well, because they helped us to evade the accusations by religious zealots and outsiders that we were "witches", during times of great persecution.

Also similar to the neo-pagan tradition, our tools are consecrated in a sense, before we use them. Unlike the Gardnerian traditions, no mythical magic circles need be cast, and the tools, even when consecrated, serve their magical and mundane purpose (with a few exceptions).

Where the Wiccan tradition uses a pentacle, in our tradition we have both a wooden cutting board. This is representative of the element of the earth, as it is both round and made from a tree, and as such, imbued with the magic of the silvani spirits. We take good care to preserve the condition of our cutting board, which can be used both as a plate (paten) and as a place on which we work (cut) the *materia magica* (as well as food). In our family, this board was never used for cutting meat, poultry or fish. Only plant matter was cut on it. *(I still have the one handed down to me from my great-great-grandmother.)*

While the Gardnerian Wicca symbol of fire was the athame (a ritual knife), in our tradition, originally, a knife was hewn from a piece of wood, which was tied with rope and refined in the moving waters of a river for a year. The one handed down to me as a young person has long since been worn down, and returned to the earth after being ritually burned and thanked for its service. These days, a professional kitchen knife is consecrated to serve in this manner, which usually bears a black handle, as would have been used by our Kemetic ancestors and Tunisian ancestors, before Sicily was our home.

The traditional Wiccan symbol for air is the wand. But for us, it's a wooden spoon, usually made of olive wood. This is used on a daily basis, and it's not uncommon for a practitioner to have dozens of wooden spoons used in the kitchen for all working, mundane and magical.

Similar to the Wiccan symbol of the element of water, which is their chalice or cup, for us, it's a bowl.

These items are often used throughout one's day, because as I pointed out, our worldview is a magical one, so while we might talk about mundane work, like cooking, versus magical work, like spellcraft, the simple fact is that our cooking is spellcraft as well. So, the tools are used for all things.

Other items that may serve specific purposes are slightly different. For example, wooden knitting needles and metal knitting needles would be the same tool used for so-called mundane knitting (if there is such a thing), but would also be used for knotwork spells, protective knitting, and so forth. But each practitioner would generally have two pair of scissors, one small and portable, and one large, kitchen sized, which is sometimes ornate. These would strictly be used for specific magical workings. We don't use them to cut coupons, or wrapping paper. They're used in breaking hexes, snipping the hair of a subject of a spell, or cutting herbal materia. Nothing else.

Some of the other items we would use might include a candle snuffer, incense holder or censer, a broom, cast iron pot and pan, and for some, a reserved bottle of olive oil (used only for things like *malocchio* removal), blessed salt, our Scopa deck of cards, red, black and white threads or twines, and red ribbon.

This may sound very simplistic to you, and if that's so, I am glad. It's historically been meant to seem simplistic, practical and for those outsiders looking for something more nefarious, well… invisible.

But you alone can determine what's indispensable for your own magical workings. Many practitioners, having been influenced or inspired by neo-pagan traditions might find a pentacle or *Mogan David* to be inspiring and useful. Others like to have the sort of wand that is spoken and written of in primitive mythology.

I am an absolute fanatic about having an electric resin burner and an essential oil diffuser on-hand at all times, because I find it energetically charges the air in a way that puts me right where I need to be, instantly.

The point is that you should not let anyone dictate to you which tools you "must have" or "must not have". I would caution about employing tools that come from traditions outside of your own, especially, if you do not know what they are intended to be used for, or have not been properly initiated into using by someone from that culture.

My family heritage is Afro-Sicilian and Hungarian-Romanian Roma. So, there are elements of both cultures in my home. My grandmothers from the Roma traditions never taught me much of their ways. On my mother's side, I was never permitted to get to know that grandmother, because she and her children were estranged. On my father's side, his mother's family were Sicilian-Neopolitans, and Roma, and my grandmother's mom was secretive about the Roma side of the tradition.

As a result, while I have always loved the wisdom, tradition, culture and aesthetic of the beautiful Romani people, I do not wear their clothing, or practice anything other than a couple very private practices I was taught, because I don't have the privilege of living within that culture, and believe that one must know their suffering to know their magic, just as I believe one must have direct heritage to African enslaved peoples, who were forcibly taken to the Americas, in order to authentically practice Hoodoo. To know their pain and suffering is to know their magic. While our common ancestors may have come from Africa at one time, I do not have melanated skin, and so I can claim no rights to their traditions and practices.

So, choose what chooses you, but be mindful not to appropriate, otherwise express your bad-ass magical self in the way that is authentic to you!

"In the final analysis, a Witch is someone whose entire being is permeated with the Craft of the Wise. This is both conscious and unconscious. Such a person is constantly studying, learning, adding and eliminating things, ever seeking new knowledge..."

Dr. Leo Martello

Anatomy of a Spell

Within different traditions, one can often find that the concept of spellcasting varies greatly. But what is common to each tradition is that something is charged with the energy that is used to set into motion the shifting of the energy around a person, place, thing, circumstance or condition, in order to influence the outcome we desire.

In certain traditions, in addition to plant materia, botanicals, elementals, planets and other celestial bodies, the ancestors and spiritual allies, there are practitioners who will use people, including the extra-dimensional beings that primitive cultures referred to as their gods, daemons, and spirits. If you were looking for that kind of spell, I am afraid to tell you that it's not part of our tradition.

We do work with extra-dimensional beings, spiritual allies, and even "distant ancestors" including those regarded as "saints" in Catholic conjure, for example. But we don't use people or these other beings as "objects" from which we draw our magic. We don't "summon" any beings of any kind, because we come from a culture of people who were enslaved themselves, and will never command another to answer to our arrogant summons.

We work with thought, first and foremost, because that is pure magic. We work with words, which are the first manifestations of thought. And then we may choose to employ the assistance and alliance of our allies — plant, spiritual, elemental, ethereal, etc.

What will follow is a direct transcription of my notes, taken down in Mystic Island, New Jersey, the summer of 1973. Vicki Lawrence was singing, "The Night the Lights Went Out in Georgia," and Helen Ready's "I Am Woman" was fast becoming the anthem of empowered women. Elton John's "Daniel," was a hit, and Wings' "Live and Let Die" was playing on the radio, with classics such as Freda Payne's "Band of Gold".

Let's stop for one moment. If you were ten years old or older in 1973, what you just likely experienced was a bit of written magic. I'm willing to be that you started hearing those songs, and feeling the feelings of that era, maybe even of that summer, as you were reading them.

At the time I was writing down "The Anatomy of a Spell", I was listening to Paul Simon's "Kodachrome", and I remember that distinctly, because I anchor the things I need to learn to music, colours or smells. And this would be the last summer my sister and I would get to spend with my beloved family matriarch, Zia Maria, her sister Zia Irenelle, and my father's mom, because my parents were moving to Florida later in the year. And I was not happy about it at all.

So just as I resolved to capture every moment of that summer down the shore, the song "Kodachrome" came on the radio, and reminded me that I could use magic to make the summer live forever in my mind. And it has.

So here's the entry, which will sound very familiar to those who have been my students, because I teach this same material the exact same way I learned it, forty-nine years ago. *(I did edit the misspellings, the frightful grammar, and bits that were less-than-clear out of it.)*

What is a spell?

- A spell is a magical formula designed to shift energy around a person, situation, condition or thing, in order to bend the outcome toward our will.

- Spells can be spoken, ritually enacted, chanted, or artistically represented.

- More properly understood in the context of incantations, the word comes from the Latin (*incantare*), which means to consecrate with one's words or thoughts. (Hmmm. So when the priest is speaking the words of the consecration at Mass, he is literally performing a spell!)

- Some of the most common types of spellwork are simple incantations or prayers, rituals, mental treatments, enjoined spellwork (*this means when more than one person works together to do the spell, like when Zia Maria helps me with protection spells for little Jeanine*), hexes and healing spells.

Incantations & Mental Treatments

- The simplest and purest form of spellcraft.

- Relies on the First Hermetic Principle.

- Based upon recognition that we are the sovereign creators of our experience.

- Serve as the foundation of all other spell work.

How Do Incantations Work?

During the process of Incantation, which the uncles refer to as Mental Treatment or Mentalism, we come to the realisation that within the universe there is one Infinite, Universal Energy/Source or Presence that permeates everything; and therefore, this Presence, being everywhere, has to be right within us, as well.

With this attitude of mind we reach an acceptance of new possibilities in life, we are able to 'see', 'feel' and speak of the good we desire as already ours. Then we let the universe work its magic.

The Steps of the Spell

So, this is the "anatomy" of the spell, step by step.

Step One: Recognition

We acknowledge that within the cosmos there is ONE pervading presence, ONE force encompassing everything that is in existence, ONE energy from which all things are made of.

Many religious and superstitious people throughout the ages have turned this Source of all things into mythological beings, giving it human characteristics, and calling it God or Goddess.

Secularists may call is Source, or simply as Zio Leo calls it, "the Magick Within". (Zia Maria gets *agita* when I put a "k" in magic, the way Zio Leo does. She says that's an Americana thing.

The name is not important, what matters is that we recognise this truth.

Step Two - Essential Unity

Having recognised that there is ONE Creative Source or Energy within the cosmos, from which all material and aetheric realities manifests, the second step is to recognise and declare our essential unity with that Source.

This is what distinguishes our tradition from the imaginary traditions upon which neo-paganism is based.

We don't believe in a "supreme being or beings", who created the cosmos. We don't personify the act of creation, nor its Source.

We therefore do not worship gods, goddesses, or any other being(s). And they have no direct role in whether or not our magic works.

Step Three - Making Your Declaration

We speak from authority, as the Sovereign Power operating within our experience, and boldly and unapologetically declare into existence that which we will. We name our desire(s) with confidence that as we do this, it is already accomplished (the Principle of Mentalism). We move away from the feeling of 'wanting' to the realisation of 'having already received'.

Step Four - Demonstration of Gratitude

Zia Maria says that this is the second most important part, and that we cannot ever do it enough. "There is never *'basta'* when it comes to gratitude."

Genuine gratitude is an organic expression that comes from knowing our working will produce the desired outcome.

The word "gratitude" comes from the Latin word *gratus*, meaning 'pleasing, thankful'.

It represents the feeling of appreciation or similar positive response shown upon the receipt of some kindness, gifts, help, favours, or other types of generosity.

Genuine gratitude opens our consciousness to receiving even more good, as the Law of the universe is such that what we focus on, is what we manifest in our experience, when we are focused on the good that we already have, then we can only attract more good.

Step Five - Release

This is the part Zia Maria and Nana says is the most important part, because without it, we remain attached to the outcome, so it cannot manifest.

"Be devoted to the working, but detached from the outcome," Mimi would tell us.

Once we have accomplished the four previous steps, all we need to do is release our word into the aether to become manifest. We release it to the wisdom and the love of the cosmos. Source does not require our input on 'how' our desire is manifesting itself for us.

We simply recognise that magic is the science and art of causing change to occur in conformity with our Will. And so we release our incantation or treatment to do the work it is intended to do.

My First Constructed Spell

So what was the first spell I created, as a neurodivergent, ten year-old kid?

I wanted it to be a spell to make my parents change their minds about moving to Florida, because I didn't understand that one of our "cousins" next to whom my dad grew up, were murdered in a mob hit, and my dad didn't want his kids growing up in that environment. But my aunt simply said, "No, we don't do spells to manipulate people. We manipulate the energy around them, and you're not ready to learn how to do something that complex right now. When you're older, you will remember this, and you will understand. So pick a new focus…"

So I chose money. And here was that spell. It's pretty simplistic, dry and nerdy, because that's how my mind operated even back then. But I can tell you that I believe this first spell set the stage for a very successful career, which included my being privileged to be one of the creators of the world's first enterprise social networks, and a hugely successful online entrepreneur, which allowed me to operate our monastic houses and AIDS clinics in the decades that followed, without ever going into debt.

"I affirm that Creative Intelligence is the Source of all supply, and that money is Source in action.

I am a perfect expression and embodiment of Source, and that Creative Energy operates in me, through me and all around me at all times.

I draw into my experience abundance, surplus, money and wealth in endless supply, which comes into my possession, and circulates from me, into the world, only to return to me multiplied.

I am grateful for this Creative Power and forgive myself and others for the times I have forgotten my ability to use this power for good.

And so I release this spell to do its good and perfect work and return to me abundantly multiplied. And so it is."

Ritual Spellwork

Ritual spellcraft operates on the same fundamental principles as incantation but employs ritual tools to serve as anchors for our energy.

These may include:

- Magically charged items, curios, talismans, and the like.

- Representations of the elements

- Hand gestures (*segnature*)

- Books or other texts

- Symbols and sigils

- Personal items

- Elements from the natural world

- Candles, burnt offerings (smoke), and sacred fires

- Poppets, murtis and relics

Enjoined Ritual Workings

In our family, we referred to this as a magical partnership or spiritual alliance. When we spoke about this type of working together, it was not the sort of group magic that one might think of in terms of the pop-culture's ceremonial magical gatherings.

For us, this enjoined magic refers to when we work with others, either human, animal or spirit to achieve a common objective.

The purpose of enjoined spellcraft is to enhance our intentionality and bolster our belief and energetic stamina to accomplish certain goals.

Enjoined spellcraft might include:

• Working with other practitioners

• Working with plant spirits

• Working with animal spirits or familiars

• Working with ancestors, saints, or the Old Ones (Fourth Dimensional beings, who may include the Original Ancestors of our people, often referred to in the African traditions as "Orishas".)

On Hexing and Baneful Work

Within our tradition, there is no such thing as "black", "grey" or "white" magic. Such distinctions are corruptions of the practice, imposed upon us by the oppressive, white, racist European culture, particularly the institutional churches of Rome and England.

Representations of race in cultural media are reflections of the society that creates them, as Douglas Kellner[5] states, "(M)edia images help shape our view of the world and our deepest values: what we consider good or bad, positive or negative, moral or evil. Media demonstrate[s] who has power and who is powerless, who is allowed to exercise force and violence and who is not. They dramatize and legitimate the power of the forces that be and show the powerless that they must stay in their places or be oppressed."

---

[5] Kellner, D. "Cultural studies, multiculturalism, and media culture." In G. Dines & J. M, 1995.

The term black magic is only a few centuries old despite its fictional pop-culture references, claiming to date back to medieval times. During the West African slave trade many of the captured Africans practiced what Christians considered pagan religions such as Voudo (Voodoo).

European Colonisers outlawed the traditional African religions and forced them to practice only their own religion. The term *black magic* was used synonymously with African religion. In the last 200 years, black magic as evolved simply to mean any magic in literature that is used for allegedly nefarious purposes.

Our tradition predates the construct of race, and therefore was never poisoned by the notions that were foundational ideas at the time of Crowley, Gardner, *et al*.

Hexes and Healing can be seen as two sides of the same coin. Our culture doesn't believe that hexing is inherently "evil", nor does it view healing as being inherently "good". We approach both hexing and healing as means of restoring balance and justice.

In either case we are working with the energy around a person, object, situation or condition, and shifting it to conform to our will to bring about homeostasis.

The Most Important Thing to Remember

All of this comes from a period in my life that was formative — not because it was when I "got the answers on how to craft a spell", but because it was when I learned that crafting a spell was truly an expression of who I am.

So it was when I realised the keys to my personal power were always in my own hands. As the years unfolded, that would sometimes mean I remembered that simple truth, and my spellcrafting was powerful and effective. Other times, I wasn't present to my power, and would flounder. And I suspect the same will prove to hold true for you. The important thing isn't that you master the anatomy of the spell as much as you recognise that within you already exists an awareness and complete understanding of that anatomy; and the mastery to use it at your own will.

Know who you are, and what you know. Devin Hunter has written what I think to be one of the most clear, insightful and potent instructional pieces about tuning back into your own power, and finding your "home frequency". In his book, The Witch's Book of Power[6], he talks about how the traditions with which we study and align ourselves connect us to a current of power, both of lineage and indwelling (soulful) source. The virtually limitless degrees of combination with which we tap into these currents/sources will influence our own experience of our innate power:

"These currents of Witch Power are unique and
specific to each tradition due to their
mythologies, core teachings, and the sources
from which they draw power. This form of Witch
Power is separate from our individual Witch
Power but informs, influences, and empowers
it... No two currents of power are ever the same,
adding much diversity to the manifestation of
ability and influence the Witch Power has."
(*The Witch's Book of Power*; Devin Hunter)

---

[6] Hunter, Devin; The Witch's Book of Power, Llewellyn Books, July, 2016 (https://amzn.to/3waRFjc)

This could be a great spot in the book to pick a time when you can just quietly sit with the information you've read, consider the information you brought with you up until this point, and allow yourself to notice those subtle, sometimes imperceptible currents of energy moving through you. Allow yourself to generate gratitude for these currents of power, because they are your own unique "thumb-print" on the magical world.

Lunar Cycles, Daily Magical Correspondences

Within the Afro-Sicilian and Southern Italian tradition, we consider ourselves to be the inheritors of the Great Lunary Mysteries, and as such, the lunar cycles play a particularly central role to our magical rhythm. And to a lesser extent, the days of the week played a role as well.

While many in the ancient world believed that the earth was at the centre of the universe, it's said that our ancestors not only understood this not to be true, but far ahead of science, believed that even with the sun appearing to be at the centre of our solar system, everything was moving, not in circles, but in a vast, arching spiral, which was projecting us across time and space.

Today, of course, we realise that this is true.

The moon phases involve three bodies in our solar system: Earth, Sun, and Moon.

While the earth spins on its axis, making a complete 360-degree rotation every 24 hours (giving us night and day), we also orbit the Sun in a yearly transit. Next, there's the Moon.

The Moon orbits Earth on its own path, making a full cycle about every 29.5 days. And of course, the Sun is the center of our solar system. It seems stationary to us, but it's also moving – our entire solar system orbits around the center of the Milky Way Galaxy. The Sun simply moves extremely slowly.

It's no coincidence that the cycles of the moon mirror the cycles within our own bodies. The same is true when we look at the cosmic dance that unfolds in the cycles of growth and harvest, death and renewal. And that is why the first consideration we make is always given to the phases of the moon -- The Mother Luna -- when we begin a specific working.

We should note that it's important not to solely consider the lunar phase with regard to specific undertakings magically, but to remember that because our worldview instills in us an awareness that we're always engaged in magic, to consider the impact of the lunar phase on even the seemingly mundane tasks.

The New Moon

The new moon is the beginning of the waxing phase of the lunar cycle. A new moon is when the Moon and Sun come back together in the sky after completing their previous cycle. The Moon appears dark -- still being infused with the light of the Sun --but not visibly from our perspective.

This is the most potent time to initiate new projects, begin working on ideas that emerge, and shift our focus and energy to new beginnings. The dark moon is full of possibility – you don't need to know how things will unfold, you just need to take action to get it started. This is the time to set intentions based on your deepest desires, release fear, lean into and trust your inner vision.

Within the Afro-Sicilian and Southern Italian tradition, we consider ourselves to be the inheritors of the Great Lunary Mysteries, and as such, the lunar cycles play a particularly central role to our magical rhythm.

While many in the ancient world believed that the earth was at the centre of the universe, it's said that our ancestors not only understood this not to be true, but far ahead of science, believed that even with the sun appearing to be at the centre of our solar system, everything was moving, not in circles, but in a vast, arching spiral, which was projecting us across time and space.

Today, of course, we realise that this is true.

We consider the New Moon to be an opportunity for intensive intention-setting. If we're going to create a powerful shift, we might set that intention on the New Moon, and ensure that we begin to prepare our homes and our interior lives to ensure that everything is in alignment with that intention.

For those who are considering a new project or new direction in their career, sitting quietly under a new moon, and making a list of the considerations, intentions and steps necessary is a powerful exercise. In our personal lives, the New Moon energy is perfect for going on first dates, or restoring the fire to an existing relationship, by setting a date night.

Energetically, the new moon is also when we take the time to cleanse our ritual space, and yes, that especially begins with our kitchens and dining tables, since those are the most prevalent ritual spaces for our tradition. But it can also extend to tidying up the ancestral altar and any areas of ritual honour in our homes.

Don't underestimate the importance of opening the windows and airing out the stagnant energy that can accumulate in the bedroom (something I recommend doing every day, but which we should give a little boost with "night air" during the new moon).

There are also points of mindfulness that can be especially useful during this New Moon energy that don't often get talked about.

Our ancestors believed that the New Moon would bring into our lives opportunities to connect with those who would be of particular importance in achieving our goals and intentional outcomes. So when an unexpected invitation or a chance to meet new people comes up during the new moon, we should never decline, unless we have strong psychic indicators that compel us to do so.

Similarly, this is not considered to be a wise time to choose to quit relationships, or walk away from a project we've been passionate about. Keep the focus of the energy on creation during this period. There will be times when we can stop something that is no longer working, and we only have to wait two weeks for that period to come.

The Waxing Crescent Moon

We begin to see evidence of the manifestation of those things we initiated under the New Moon, as the Mother Luna enters her waxing crescent phase.

I liken this to planting seeds for our favourite plant. Those feelings we experience when the first shoots break through the soil, and we see evidence that our intention are manifesting, we are filled with all the desires and commitments to take care of and tend to the nurturing of those seedlings, to help them become mature and beautiful plants.

So too should we use the Waxing Crescent energy to draw upon our resolve and and commitments to see our intentions through to their meaningful outcomes.

Schedule meetings, or put into place the structures needed to realise your intentions. Notice the arising feelings of that nurturing Mother Energy within yourself, and harness its intuitive power.

The First Quarter

The First Quarter-Phase of the lunar cycle does not mean that only a quarter of the moon is visible (that's the Waxing Crescent).

It means one-quarter of *the full cycle of the moon* has completed, and so that means we see *half of the moon*, in all her splendor.

Imagine going on a cruise, on an incredible ship from an obscure little island, headed toward the breathtaking South Pacific Bora Bora - French Polynesia's crown jewel. You're halfway there, and can see the incredible views of the island.

That is the first-quarter of the lunar phase.

You don't take in that breathtaking view and then say, "OK, I've seen it... I'm halfway there. Let's turn around and go home!"

Instead, you redouble your commitment, maybe even change clothes and freshen up, and put all your energy toward reaching that desired outcome. The first quarter moon is a time for taking stock, being critical of your approach, refining areas that might need to be refined, and then setting out to realise your goals.

In our more mundane tasks, we approach them with the awareness that our magical workings have been released into the aetheric realm, and so we ensure that our surroundings, our relationships, our homes and our lives are prepared for the accomplishment of the working. Are we ready to step into that outcome? And if not, what can we do to become ready.

The Waxing Gibbous (Three-Quarter Full) Moon

Going back to our analogy of our traveling to Bora Bora, we're now just a couple hundred yards from the shore. And in my imagining of the scene, as I approach, a scantily-clad, Lil Nas X is waiting for me, surrounded by twenty or thirty equally-hot attendants, and a smile that's as bright as the reflection of the sun on the shimmering Chrysler Building's chromed exterior.

What do I do? Do I leave to chance my own appearance? Or do I make sure that my hygiene, my appearance and everything else that he will be greeted with as we approach that shore is absolutely as well-prepared as possible?

Notice, I didn't shoot for everything being perfect, but for everything I could possibly do to support the outcome I desire being in place.

That is how we harness the power of the Waxing Gibbous Moon. We tweak the edges *(and maybe a nipple)* to ensure we're as ready as possible for the full manifestation of our desired outcomes. We avoid fixating on the things beyond our control. We lean-into the moment, and the enthusiasm and excitement carry us through those final days to the complete radiance of the Full Moon that approaches.

The Full Moon

When the moon is new, we set our intentions and charge them with the energy of creation. When she is full, we give birth to that creation in our experience.

The Full Moon is the culmination point of the entire wave of waxing lunar energy. And so it's the point at which we allow ourselves to relax into gratitude for all that we have manifested.

This is not a time to seek new beginnings, or to initiate intense discussions. It's a time for letting go. During this lunar phase, we take care not to overextend ourselves. We guard against the "craziness" of the energy that often can bring us intensive insights, and so we avoid intoxication, we avoid rushing, and we don't allow ourselves to bet thrown off by the tendency the Full Moon can have to magnify our emotions and awareness.

This is the perfect opportunity for us to again sit quietly, as we did on the New Moon, but this time, we take inventory of the things which may be troubling us, weighing us down, or holding us back. We consider how much different our lives could be if we made one or two powerful changes, and let go of the anger, the fear or the uncertainty that is holding us back.

Full Moon energy is a period for allowing forgiveness to flow through us and circulate all around us. It's all about letting the negative emotions and negative energy be released.

If there are relationships or situations we need to let go of, this is the time for doing that. If we're ready to change directions, or leave a dead-end job, again this is the time for doing that.

Full moons allow us the space to let go of projects that no longer serve us. And it can be useful in our daily lives to notice the things in our homes that surround us, and during the full moon, to get rid of that which no longer serves a useful purpose in our lives.

Nicole Kincaid is a graduate from Cal Poly San Luis Obispo and Bastyr University, whose training in social science, spirituality, health and medicine led her on a journey to become one of the most gifted and insightful energy workers I've had the honour of meeting. Nicole specialises in helping people fall in love with their spaces in this world, by also helping them let go of that which no longer serves them. Her Stuffology approach (cf: https://nicolekincaid.com/) is something which I think embodies the energy of the Full Moon in one of the most powerful and breathtaking ways I could ever imagine.

Because the full Moon is considered the "energetic peak" of the month, it's the perfect time to tap into its power and practice a little self-care. So this is when we ground ourselves, indulge a bit, and look inwardly. But it's another time when we pay special attention to the opportunities that we have to cleanse and clear our physical space, deepening our connection to that magical rhythm that our ancestors understood so deeply.

The Full Moon embodies self-expression and action, representing completion, illumination and celebration.

Ask yourself what that means for you, and then act on it.

The Waning Gibbous Moon

Within our tradition, the Waning Gibbous Moon is often called the Ancestral Moon, because this is a period set aside when we place special importance on showing the ancestors our gratitude for all that they do each moment of our lives to influence, inspire and align us with our Highest Potential.

During the Waning Gibbous phase of the moon, the ancestors will surely let us know what needs to be released, if we haven't already begun to do so, and will set the stage for us to take action on it.

This is considered to be a powerful time for doing banishing spells, protection work, and intensive spiritual cleansing. Our ancestors and spiritual allies will work in tandem with us toward these ends, when we begin such work at during this lunar phase.

During this phase, I prefer to do divination specifically-focused on tuning into my ancestors, and asking them to come through on anything I am not paying attention to. And I always start and end this work by simply demonstrating my profound and intense gratitude for their presence in my life and in my work.

The Last Quarter Phase (Waning Half Moon)

During the Waning Half Moon, we're sailing away from the shores of what no longer serves us. It's not at all uncommon for us to experience a crisis of "what-ifs" as I call it.

Because we are leaving behind all that no longer serves us, one of the biggest things we're potentially leaving behind, if we've done the work, is our fear. And that fear often has deep roots.

So energetically, it may feel like something is being ripped out of us or ripped away... and it is... But despite our imagining that what's being ripped away is part of us, it never was.

And once we surrender to it being ripped away, the soil of our souls and minds is suddenly aerated. The roots of that fear leave behind spaces in which we can actually begin to grow.

We become freed from the attachments that were the foundations of the prison bars that were holding us back, during this previous lunar cycle, and we're ready to move into the magic of endings.

Therefore, if you are seeking retribution or justice, this lunar phase will help you find peace in knowing that the ancestral spirits are working with you to bring truth to light in all matters. So, it's a final opportunity to let go of the anger, the fear, and the beliefs that no longer serve us.

The Balsamic Moon (Waning Crescent)

In Italy, balsamic vinegar was believed to have restorative and healing properties. And that is why we refer to the Waning Crescent Moon as being balsamic. Its energy is the energy of restoration and healing.

It's when we lean into the shadow, and therein discover greater truths about ourselves. The last vestiges of our attachments and whatever no longer serves us deteriorates and falls away. We turn our energetic work toward personal development, insight awareness, and restoration of our personal sovereignty.

A Set Stage

Astrologer Narayana Montúfar tells us, "Lunar magic is important for many different reasons. Since the moon rules our most basic needs—like nurturing, sleeping patterns, fertility, and subconscious mind—when these are out of sync, only lunar magic can help us get back in touch with our inner child as a way to balance our feminine energy."

Daily Correspondences

Just as the lunar cycle was a central part of our magical rhythm, we've seen in the first chapter, when discussing the foods eaten on specific days of the week, as a means of informing and reinforcing our mindful magical practice, that the days of the week were regarded as having specific magical influences that could enhance our working.

By better understanding the correspondent attributes of each day of the week, we can become a bit more adept at tuning into the energies of that day to enhance our spiritual efforts.

During the years of my academic research, I found that there was a great deal more detailed attention placed on this aspect of our practice in the traditions that were more stella and solar oriented, than in the Afro-Sicilian and Southern Italian traditions.

For our ancestors, the general awareness and understanding of the energies and planetary correspondences were enough, and for me, that continues to work.

Sunday

Name Origin – The Sun

Planet – The Sun

Colours – Gold and Yellow

Crystals – Topaz, Sun Stone, Amber, Quartz, Diamond, Carnelian, Tigers Eye

Herbs – Marigold, Calendula, Sunflower, Cinnamon, St. John's Wort, Frankincense

Associations – Success, Prosperity, Fame, Wealth, Promotion, Miracles, Healing, Strength

On Sundays, we "plant seeds" -- not just material crops or plants, but also metaphysical, energetic and magical "intentional" seeds.

Monday

Name Origin – The Moon

Planet – The Moon

Colours – White, Silver, Pearl, Light Blue, Light Grey

Crystals – Moonstone, Opal, Pearl, Selenite, Aquamarine

Herbs – Willow, Lotus, Chamomile, Catnip, Wintergreen, Mint, Sage, Comfrey

Associations – Intuition, Women's Mysteries, Fertility, Dreaming, Sleep, Illusion, Femininity, Peace, Spirituality, Justice

Monday's lunar connection makes it particularly potent and auspicious to begin all things spiritual and justice oriented.

Tuesday

Name Origin – Germanic God Tiu

Planet – Mars

Colours – Red, Pink, Orange, Black

Crystals – Bloodstone, Flint, Garnet, Ruby, Rhodonite

Herbs – Holly, Coneflower, Cactus, Thistles, Basi

Associations – War, courage, Rebellion, Success, Strength, Protection, Conflict

On Tuesday, we resolve conflicts, internally and externally, and we strengthen our relationships and health.

Wednesday

Name Origin – Woden's Day

Planet – Mercury

Colours – Yellow, Orange, Purple, Magenta

Crystals – Agates, Citrine, Aventurine,

Herbs – Lillies, Lavender, Fern, Aspen, Eucalyptus

Associations – Business, The Arts, Chance, Creativity, Fortune, Debt, Transportation, Wisdom, Healing, Communication, Contracts, Music, Education

Wednesdays are all about our business and financial success. This is a good day to do a working to open up lines of communication—especially if your actions are preventing you from being an effective speaker or listener. And it's a day that is auspicious for entering into or severing our business agreements.

Thursday

Name Origin – Thor

Planet – Jupiter

Colours – Royal Blue, Green, Purple

Crystals – Lapis Lazuli, Amethyst, Turquoise, Lepidolite, Sugilite

Herbs – Oak, Cinquefoil, Honeysuckle, Melissa, Clove, Sage

Associations – Honor, Wealth, Healing, Harvest, Prosperity, Abundance, Loyalty, Business, Travel, Merchants, Education

Thursdays were often "payday" for our ancestors, and so it's a day when the fruits of our work are demonstrated. It is also the day in which we honour our ancestral oaths of allegiance and loyalty to our traditions.

Friday

Name Origin – Frigga

Planet – Venus

Colours – Pink, Grey, White, Aqua

Crystals – Jade, Coral, Rose Quartz, Emerald, Lapis Lazuli, Coral, Malachite

Herbs – Feverfew, Apple Blossoms, Strawberries, Cardamon, Saffron

Associations – Love, Romance, Passion, Fertility, Birth, Pregnancy, Friendship, Alliances, Grace, Balance, Prosperity

Deeper, more intimate or hidden alliances are associated with Friday.

Saturday

Name Origin – The God Saturn

Planet – Saturn

Colours – Black, Grey, Red, Dark Purple

Crystals – Obsidian, Hematite, Apache Tear, Jet, Serpentine

Herbs – Cypress, Mullein, Thyme, Black Poppy Seeds

Associations – Wisdom, Spirituality, Cleansing, Protection, Banishing, Psychic Attack, Self-discipline

Saturday's are when those who dared to "fuck around" with us finally "find out".

Candle Preparation & Ritual Work

Candle magic is a form of magic that uses the power of candles to manifest desires. This type of magic is not only limited to burning candles, but also includes the use of candle colours and the ritual dressing of candles, often referred to as "fixing" the candle, with herbs, *materia magica* and other ingredients.

Candle magic has been around for centuries and is still used by people in a variety of ways today. Candle magic can be used as a way to heal oneself, or as a way to bring about change in one's life.

All of this said, it's important to realise that the use of candles in our tradition is a relatively late addition. This is likely because it was not something easily come by, and presented some greater risk that working around a fire or an indoor hearth. In the ancient world, beeswax would have been a rare, luxury item. So tallow candles, made from animal fat, and not terribly pleasant in fragrance would have been the alternative.

Pouring through volumes of family writings, the earliest mention of using candles in spells came from the early 20th century. And those were usually spells done around the types of magic we would refer to as "Catholic Conjure".

Still for those who want a guide to working with candles today, I will share some of the best practices, because I will freely admit to becoming a bit crazed when I see new age, pop-culture "insta-witches" recommending that people drop crystals into glass candles (potential projectile fire hazards in the making!) or those who show themselves liberally "dressing" the outside of a candle with essential oils, and then abruptly ending the video when their entire bedroom vanity is on fire from foolish lack of respect for the element of fire.

I recommend five important steps when doing candle magic, which can then serve as the foundation of all sorts of workings:

- Step One: Choose the appropriate type and colour candle that corresponds with the working you will undertake. For simple ritual work, a tea-light or small votive candle is suitable, or even the sort of candle one might find in a holiday menorah.

- Step Two: Invite the element of fire to be your spiritual ally in the working. If you have not cultivated a relationship with fire for a minimum of six months, then doing candle magic is likely not your best choice. Ask the elemental to assist in you maintaining the safety of the working. Invite the element of water to surround and protect your working, as a means of supporting the passion of the fire element, and containing your magic within safe bounds. You can accomplish this easily by placing your candle inside a weighted glass candle holder (votive holder or pillar container) and setting it within a larger bowl of spring water.

- Step Three: Charge the candle. Energetically imbue your candle with the charge of your intention. This can be done as simply as holding the unlit candle, breathing your intention over it, or carving into the candle a symbol that represents the work you're about to undertake.

- Step Four: Dress/fix the candle. If you are working with a candle contained in a glass holder, crushed herbal material may carefully be added to the top. Preferably, preparing those herbal allies on a plate on which the bowl of water and candle itself are placed, so that no chance of burning off the materia magica until the very end will provide for a safer experience, thus allowing your focused concentration to go unbroken.

- Step Five: When there are less than ten minutes of burn-time left for your candle ritual, it's a good time to crush up the plant materia, and if necessary, the stated intention (if it was written on paper or on a leaf) and burn it off in the candle. I've never felt like this was necessary, unless I was using bay leaf, on which I would sometimes write a word or symbol. Again, exercise fire safety and common sense. And safely dispose of the burned candle, NEVER blowing it out. (Allow it to extinguish naturally, or use a snuffer.)

Candle Colours

- White: promotes serenity and peace and enhances personal strength and insight. White candles can also be used as a substitution for all other colours.

- Black: for psychic protection. Absorbing energy. Binding. Banishing. Shadow work.

- Green: helps bring your ideas to life and amplifies prosperity, partnerships and peace.

- Blue: connects with your chakras and any emotional wounds that need healing. Communication, dreamwork and social justice.

- Yellow: enhances your networking and social skills, bringing in new career opportunities. (Try keeping one on your desk—unlit.)

- Red: encourages love, sex, and passion. Also used for assertiveness, overcoming obstacles.

- Pink: This one's for romance. Placing a pink candle by your home's doorway will welcome in love. Represents sensuality and healing of physical abuse.

- Purple: boosts your spiritual enlightenment and creativity. Psychic protection, writing, sovereignty.

- Orange: encourages your ambition and helps you broaden your horizons. Pure attraction energy. Get yours!

- Brown: helps with all things relating to your personal and material resources (like health, energy, possessions, endurance, and courage). Also helps with grounding and finding lost objects.

I think I would round out this chapter by simply encouraging you to be yourself, and let the magic express itself as an extension of who you are.

As Natasha Helvin writes:

"Believe in yourself, and you will find that you are

surrounded by real magic.

Accept who you really are, and you will discover

a magic in it purest form.

Embrace your inner energy and radiate your

spiritual strength. Liberate yourself

because you are the most powerful

tool in your life. You ARE the magic!"

CHAPTER FOUR

Spellcrafting

Working With the Spells in this Book

Another dearly loved and respected member of my extended Queer magical tribe, Storm Faerywolf, recently released a new book, entitled "The Satyr's Kiss: Queer Men, Sex Magic and the Modern Craft[7]". Like the incredible books by his partners, Chas Bogan, Mat Auryn, and Devin Hunter, Storm represents one of the best examples I could think of to demonstrate why I will always remain an ally to those who find ways to take magical traditions, and make them more culturally relevant, meaningful and contemporary. And they are but a handful of the dozens of neo-pagan practitioners for whom I have nothing but love and respect.

It's easy to look at all the ways our spellwork and magical worldview might differ. It's petty and commonplace to explore how some of us have rejected the patheons of old, and others have abandoned the personal deity construct altogether. But what inspires me is when I find someone who's sleeves are rolled up and who's deeply entrenched in doing the work. And Storm is one of those.

I had to scramble to have this rewrite added to this manuscript, because there was a section of his book that I just felt needed to be mentioned in this grimoire. Storm points out that spells are often meant to be read as poetry with the understanding that the poetry itself is part of the spell:

---

[7] The Satyr's Kiss: Queer Men, Sex Magic and the Modern Craft, Storm Faerywolf, Llewellyn Publications, 2022 - https://amzn.to/3mYD1Gu

To read a spell, especially to do so aloud, is a potent tool to help shift our consciousness into another realm, what I often refer to as "the state of Enchantment." It is here that we are in "Faeryland," that mystical state in which, according to the folklore as well as modern practice, we can commune with the unseen world and work in tandem toward our goals.

Storm Faerywolf, *"The Satyr's Kiss"*, Chapter 11

Now I want to take this moment to thank the editor I woke up at midnight, on a Thursday, to beg her to let me email a couple paragraphs that absolutely needed to be included at the top of this chapter; because I am well aware that her eyes likely rolled in her head, when she saw what all the fuss was about, at first. But I can assure you that once it sat with her a bit, the next afternoon, she sent me a text that said she was glad I added that, and couldn't stop thinking about spells as poetry first.

You see, I needed to include that, because it was something I had been spending hours trying to express, earlier in the month, when I struggled to find a way to tie together this entire third section of my grimoire.

My grandmother — the one who referred to her family's Romani background as there having been "wandering minstrels" — always said that I was the family's poet. She referred to me as a tribal bard, and believed that those of us who were genderqueer were always the ones who were drawn to serve in that way.

From childhood, despite being told that spells didn't have to rhyme, I was the one child for whom it came naturally to develop a poetic meter in my spellcraft. And while I understood that I was being told that the spells "didn't have to rhyme" as a means of expressing that our magic didn't have to rhyme, I was also keenly aware that when they rhymed, there was magic in the rhyming itself. And Storm expressed that in the perfect words.

And so, we're going to begin to dive into spellwork in this section, which I have tried my very best to keep somewhat organised, based on how the reader might want to use it. Now, as you're reading it; however, I would like to remind you that the spells will be coming from about 37 different notebooks, Books of Secrets, various letters and other correspondence gathered over the past fifty years of my life.

As a result, some of it will be a little rough and rudimentary. Others might be more polished, and without question, there will be a few really cheesy moments with the Bard of Broad Street, yours truly, attempting to be poetic at age 16, 20, and 24.

Going through all these books and letters, I have come to experience another kind of magic as well...

The magic that happens when we look back at the things we've learned and get that rare glimpse of magic-in-motion over a lifetime; because it's in these moments that we rediscover our voice.

In his book, *The Books of Magic: The Invisible Labyrinth*, in which author Neil Gaiman brings together some favourites from the D.C. Comic Universe, including Dr. Occult and Constantine to help Timothy Hunter come to terms with and choose his destiny as a powerful magician, Gaiman writes: "Magic is a method of talking to the universe in words that it cannot ignore."

And that is indeed what this section of spells are... means of talking to the universe in words that it cannot (and will not) ignore.

Each spell I've included has been one that I have personally used, usually multiple times, before I was confident enough to include them in my later Books of Secrets. They're all from the Afro-Sicilian and Southern Italian tradition of my people, but have surely been influenced by all of the cultures that helped Sicily become Sicily over the aeons.

I've largely dispensed with the notion of using traditional or precise methods of measuring. The only exceptions will be when I offer formulas for teas, salves, balms, oils and ointments that use essential oils.

The reason for this is the reason I've seldom released cookbooks, despite frequent requests for me to do so. I don't measure. I don't write down precise measurements. And I seldom do something the same way twice. Not when I am cooking, and not when I am doing spellwork.

Also, it is implied that before undertaking any spell in this section, the practitioner makes it a priority to take a cleansing bath or shower, quiet themselves and ground themselves in their home frequency, in the present moment, and have made offerings to the ancestors and the spirits with whom they will be seeking alliance in the working.

There will be a separate section that covers this after the spell section, within the context of ritual work.

CHAPTER FIVE

Banishment

Banishing magic is a type of spell which can be used to remove something or someone from a particular situation or place, with the explicit intention that their removal be permanent.

Banishing spells can be used to get rid of anything from negative thoughts and emotions to bad habits. They are also often used in rituals for protection. Banishing spells can be found in many different cultures, including Celtic, Native American, and African cultures.

Some banishing spells use objects such as herbs or stones to represent the thing that needs to be banished. Other banishing spells use symbols, such as pentagrams or hexagrams. A symbol may also be drawn on the ground with salt and water; this is called a "smudging" spell. The idea behind these types of banishing spells is that if you get rid of the object or symbol representing what you want to ban, and its physical correspondence in the material world is simultaneously banished.

Archaeological and anthropological evidence points to the ancient practitioners of Sicily and Southern Italy employing "curse tablets" -- spells written on lead, wax or stone -- inscribed by those who felt they had been brought harm, injury or disrespect. The curse tablet could then be given to the local practitioner, who would complete the banishment or hex.

One such tablet, inscribed by the victim, Docilinus, invokes the spiritual alliance of Mercury to bring a curse upon Varianus, Peregrina and Sabinianus, who were accused of bringing harm to someone's livestock.

"I ask that you drive them to the greatest death, and do not allow them health or sleep unless they redeem from you what they have administered to me," cursed the aggrieved Docilinus.

In the Afro-Sicilian tradition, we would also include spells under this classification, which would banish "causes and conditions" from us, for example, banishing negative energy or the "force of depression" from our experiences.

North African practitioner, Sera L puts it this way: "Banishing happens through personal strength, mindfulness, clearly speaking your demands, and bold acts of honesty. This tool requires existing in the moment, encouraging you to move through time towards the future and your ever-growing grace and strength. Our emotions bend and shift our awareness, and time changes with it. To live within reality in a balanced way, we have to begin at the emotional level."

Banishing Dust & Banishing Oil

Don't get excited... this isn't a spell to prevent you from ever having to dust your furniture again!

Banishing Dust is a staple in a number of Afro-Sicilian spells, and serves as the base for creating Banishing Oil and Banishing Water as well.

One of the most important components of Banishing Dust is sulfur, which was naturally occurring in the land surrounding Mt. Vesuvius, in various forms, both plant and mineral based. My aunts would tell me the "easiest source to come by" was gypsum, which is very similar to blackboard chalk.

Banishing Powder

- Gypsum powder

- Ground bay leaves

- Dried Hydrangea flowers

- Dried rue (ruta graveolens)

- Black pepper powder

- Sea salt

The use of this powder in its natural form, which would be made on the first night after the Full Moon, and allowed to sit for nine nights under the waning moon energy, would vary.

Because it's potent, just a pinch is needed, making it an exceptional powder for "hiding in plain sight".

This is how my grandmother taught us to use it (taken from my journals at age 14):

"Take a pinch of the dust in your left hand, between the first three fingers. Walk around the subject you wish to banish counter-clockwise, stopping briefly behind them, and while talking or spinning an animated story, gently touch their shoulder, releasing some of the powder on their clothing. When the time comes from them to leave, take another pinch, also in the left hand, and as they leave, walk a step or two behind them, dropping the powder into their footsteps. After they're no longer in sight, open the door to your home, and pass the broom (sweep) from where they were sitting, out the door and at least nine steps away from the home."

Banishing Oil

Banishing Oil is made on the night of the Balsamic Moon, by taking three pinches of Banishing Dust, and adding it to a 30-40ml bottle, into which equal parts of sunflower and castor oil are added. An eighth tsp of vodka or grain alcohol is added, and the whole thing mixed up and allowed to "cure" for 30 days. Discard after six months.

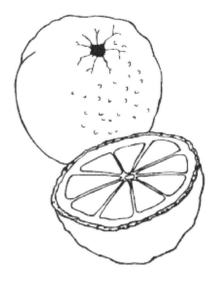

The most common use of this oil is to create a small "oil candle", by taking a blood orange or bergamot, and cutting off the top third. Carefully take the fruit out, leaving the centre "thread" of the orange intact and attached to the bottom of the orange.

You will be left with a "shell" made of the orange skin, forming a "votive bowl" with a centre-stem wick. In a small demitasse cup, add in nine drops of Banishing Oil mixed with sunflower oil, and fill the orange "votive". Light the wick, and allow it to burn on the table (in a fireproof dish or bowl) for three hours.

An alternative method of doing this involves allowing some coffee grounds to fall into the subject's coffee cup, which they would be served, while visiting you. Once they leave, and ensuring that they are out of sight, gather some dirt from one of their footprints on the path leaving your home. Dump this, and their coffee grounds from their cup into the orange rind before filling it with the oil, and allow to burn for three hours, seeing them stay far from you forever in your mind's eye.

Banishing Gossip

A pot or two of beautiful *lobelia* -- an attractive annual with purple and blue flowers -- should always be kept in a sunny spot outside your front door.

This plant does better in the warmer regions.

But even throughout the winter, a sprig of lobelia root would be found in a charm bag, in my family's pockets or purses, and a sprig of the root, tied with a red ribbon to a *cimaruta* could be found above the door.

The reason for this is that the leaves and flowers reduce inflammation, while the root when ingested will cause nausea and "gagging". The idea being that those who speak well of you will "breathe easy" and those who have your name on their lips with malevolent intent will gag on their words.

Candle Magic - Banishing Spell

This particular spell can be used to banish people, situations or conditions.

Ingredients:

- Black candle
- Bowl of sea salt mixed with black pepper

- Match sticks (preferred to a lighter, since matches contain sulfur)

- Lobelia root

- Banishing oil

Ritual:

1. Call the subject of your banishing spell to mind, and carve into the candle a word or symbol (sigil) to represent your intention.

2. Anoint the wick of the candle with a drop of the banishing oil, and place into a bowl of sea salt.

3. Sprinkle black pepper into the salt in a counter-clockwise direction, saying:

Turn away, or face the knife,

I banish you now from my life.

4. Allow the candle to completely burn down.

Banishing Bad Habits

Banishing need not be limited to people. As I mentioned at the beginning of this chapter, we can also banish circumstances, including bad habits.

My cousin, who was six years older than me, shared this spell with me, which our aunts taught him a few years earlier. He and I shared a bedroom at our aunts' home on the Jersey Shore each summer, and he was the first person in whom I confident about my attraction to males.

There was a particular guy, around my age, on whom I had a serious crush. Bobby told me that the aunts told him how to work this spell himself a couple years earlier, when his "panty-chasing" was getting him into trouble at home, at school, and down the shore.

It's a spell that will work on all bad habits or obsessive behaviours. It is only done between the New Moon and at least three nights before the Full Moon.

Things you need

- White candle
- Bay leaves
- Sage
- Rosemary
- Cloves
- Lavender
- Incense
- A cast-iron cauldron (or a pan)
- A pen
- Paper

How it's done

The first thing you need to do is to quiet and settle your mind, rooting yourself deeply in the present moment.

After that light a white candle.

Take your cauldron and burn bay leaves, sage, rosemary, cloves, lavender and incense in it. They have to burn down before you can continue.

Take small pieces of paper and, with a black pen, write on each one a thing you want to eliminate from your life, drawing a black dot near it.

Here are examples:

Beat down envy, jealousy, laziness, obstacles, economic problems, loneliness, etc. Do not direct this toward people! Instead, write what bothers you about that person, like nastiness, jealousy, revenge, evil eye, etc.

For each piece of paper written, hold the slip of paper and say:

"Mother of the Moon who breaks down the darkness,

erases misfortune and negativity.

Banish this black point from this house and from my heart you have to banish it."

Then bring the paper to the flame and, as soon as it catches fire, throw it into the cauldron, repeating your formula.

When you have exhausted the sheets, remember to close your ritual with gratitude for the Mother of the Moon being your spiritual ally in this working.

If the pieces of paper are struggling to burn completely, it means that there are blocks.

If something like this happens, make sure to recast the spell, perhaps waiting three days and pondering whether you truly are ready to banish whatever it is from your experience.

Send Them Far, Far Away

Take a small matchbox, leaving three matches inside for their sulfur content. On a slip of paper or bay leaf, write the name of the person you want to go away, folding it away from you, and placing it inside the box. Close the box and wrap the box shut with red twine or thread, crosswise, saying:

You might have come, but cannot stay.

It's time for you to go away.

The water's current you cannot fight,

as life takes you far from my sight.

Place the box in a river, stream or ocean, and allow it to be carried away. Be sure to thank the spirits of the water (the *manii*) for helping you with this working.

The Meddling Nuisance

From time to time, there are people who just seen to bring meddling energy to our lives. It may be the nosy neighbour, or the meddlesome in-law. Maybe it's that person we suspect is always trying to get into ours or our loved one's pants.

This is one way to send them on their way that will never fail:

Mix 1/2 graveyard dirt, and half cayenne pepper in a small, discrete envelope. Add in a pinch of sea salt and spit three times into the mix.

On a Dark Moon, pour the mixture into your toilet and then pee on it, as you think of all the reasons you want that person to stay away.

A final word on banishment…

Banishing can be applied to energetic spaces, objects, people, situations, spirits, behaviors, shadow work, etc. If something can change, and no longer exist in your life, then it can be banished.

A Few Thoughts on Banishing Work

An excerpt from my personal "Book of Secrets" (grimoire) when I was sixteen:

If our lives truly are, as I believe, an expression of the beliefs we hold, the thoughts we entertain, and quite often, a projection of the subconscious fears, anxieties and unresolved hurt that we carry with us, then it would be a serious offense to disadvantage ourselves by not taking full responsibility for the life we've lived and experienced thus-far.

Now, of course I don't mean that we're responsible for everyone else's behaviour. And I am not saying we need to blame ourselves, when something terrible occurs. But what if there were really no limits to the extent to which we can alter this iteration of the multiverse? What if everything that's happening is part of the cosmos responding to the data we're feeding into the "holodeck" (our fears, beliefs, expectations and magical workings), so that these experiences, and to some extent, the behaviours of others, is somehow linked to the implicate order of things after all?

If that is the case, shouldn't it impact the way we approach things like banishing spells?

In fact, shouldn't it impact every aspect of our magical tradition?

What if banishing is simply laying down that energetic imprint on the fabric of this present reality, to "mark" the occasion, the way we take note of how many minutes into a concerto the second

112

movement begins? What if the banishment itself is the moment we realise (and as such, take back our power and recognise) that this experience in life is entirely within our control, and that the cosmos is simply responding to our programming.

And so, if we want a better experience, we need to input better beliefs, expectations, and data.

I am beginning to see that the ancestors understood this, but didn't always have the words for it.

CHAPTER SIX

Binding Spells

Binding spells are workings that restrain someone metaphysically, and are best performed during the full or waning moon.

Not all binding spells are negative in their intentions. They can be done to prevent someone from doing harm to themselves or to others.

It's important to understand that when a binding spell is performed, there is an energetic attachment created, binding that person and the practitioner together. In popular culture, especially among Wiccan practitioners, an imaginary distinction arises between "binding spells" and "being bound and restrained" magically. But this distinction is purely pop-culture fiction, and demonstrative of an inexperience with actual magical binding.

Regardless of whether you're intentionally binding someone to you, in order to preserve or strengthen a relationship bond, as with the practice of handfasting, or binding a person to prevent them from doing harm, you're creating a metaphysical "bond".

Some will debate the ethics of doing such things without another person's permission, or against their will. That is outside the scope of this grimoire. I make no ethical judgments on how others choose to use this information, reserving such things for my own conscience and my own use of these spells.

It is not my personal belief that we can impose our will on another entirely. I believe that free will is a reality, and in the sovereignty of each sentient being on the planet.

However, I also believe that when properly motivated, a binding spell will allow us to energetically connect with and attach to the place within the subject, which knows that something is for their highest and greatest good.

There is a long history in the practices of binding spells, which likely came to our culture through the ancient Greeks and Minoans. We know that the ancient Greeks utilised binding, which they called *katadesmos*, often by creating curse tablets or spell tablets.

In the Afro-Sicilian tradition, we're told that our ancestors would inscribe the name of the intended target upon parchment, using their blood or urine, and then pierce the paper with a coffin nail, then depositing it in a grave, where the spirits of the dead would enforce the spell, binding them to our will.

In more recent history, it's said that a group under the instruction of Wiccan founder, Gerald Gardner, performed a binding spell upon Hitler and his troops, to prevent their invasion of England, in 1941.

As a rule, I recommend that you not bind someone for whom you have nothing but hatred, or someone you don't know at all. Such persons would be far better banished than bound.

Reserve binding magic for those you care about, whose welfare you ultimately seek to preserve. It's just cleaner.

Sure, I understand the mythology behind the Gardnerian ritual to bind Hitler. And I understand how human emotion can tempt us to want to bind those who have done harm to us and our loved ones. I'm not saying that I wouldn't seriously hex and curse someone who did such things to me or mine. I am simply saying that I wouldn't necessarily bind them. There are better ways that prevent any attachment to me energetically.

Remember this...

If you bind someone to you, that attachment you've created can be used by them (or another, more skillful practitioner) against you. It becomes a point of vulnerability, and I was taught never to create points of vulnerability, or opportunities for reversal in my magic. This has served me well. And it will serve you well also.

Binding from Doing Harm

Simple Candle Spell to Bind Someone from Doing Harm

Ingredients:

- White candle, engraved with the subject's name.

- Honey

- Dried rose petals

- Cinnamon

- Rue

- Bowl of sea salt

Ritual:

1. Smear the surface of the candle with a small amount of honey.

2. On a plate, mix dried rose petals, cinnamon, and rue.

3. Roll candle in the mixture and allow to dry for three hours, placing it upright in a bowl of sea salt.

4. Perform the spell nine minutes after moonrise for nine consecutive nights.

5. Light the candle. Place both hands in the air. Speak loud and clear, "From doing harm, or causing pain, I bind you now and speak your name. [State the person's name]".

6. Repeat this three times.

7. Now say as loud as possible, "I've said these words of binding, and so now it shall be." Clap your hands together, into a *prayer mudra* (*namaste* gesture) as hard as possible. Repeat this final chant three times.

Sotto una Roccia (Under a Rock)

There are times you may wish to bind someone, in a way that is non-permanent. For example, when someone is behaving like an ass, and you just want to keep them from disrupting your life. There may not be a need to permanently bind them, and so we temporarily bind them by "placing them under a rock".

This is accomplished by taking an ordinary rock, so long as it is not made of quartz or any other precious gemstone. Take time to connect gratefully with the earth, and ask that the spirits of the earth assist you in keeping those placed under this rock from creating harm, disruption and chaos in your life and the lives of those you love.

I keep this rock somewhere that is unobtrusive, and not readily apparent to those who may be at or in my home.

Whenever the need arises, I take a post-it note, inscribe it with the name of the person I wish to bind, and then write the words, "*Sotto una roccia!*" (literally, *under a rock*) across the name (twice, forming an X across their name).

I fold the paper toward me, and then again, into quarters, and I take it to the rock. I place the paper under the rock, and lay the rock back on top of it forcefully, saying, "Sotto una roccia!" three times.

Mirror Binding

This binding spell takes cunning and care to pull off, but when done properly is stunningly quick. Using a hand-held mirror, such as a cosmetic compact or a table mirror, catch the target's face in the mirror without them noticing.

Immediately say:

"Freedom's lost and now unwitting,

into this glass you'll do my bidding."

The small mirror should then be wrapped in black cloth and bound by a black ribbon or cord when not in use.

To Resolve and Bind People Who are Negative Influences

Whenever there is someone who seems to bring chaos and drama with them into your space, you can easily bind them immediately upon their leaving.

Light frankincense and nag champa incense, as soon as they're out the door, and then take a black string, cord or ribbon, holding it in both hands, and acknowledge the role you may play in having allowed this person into your home. Take back your power and bind them so that they can never unsettle the peaceful energy in your home, which you should now feel as the nag champa and frankincense purify the space.

Tie one knot in the middle of the cord, saying, "Negativity here be bound," and then tie a knot at the left of it, near the end saying, "Untoward drama do confound," and finally to the right of the centre knot, near the other end, make a final knot, saying, "Vulnerable moments won't be found."

Place this cord above the hearth or on a spot of the kitchen table, where it won't be disturbed for three days. (If your home is busy, it can be placed inside a book and placed on a shelf where no one is likely to disturb it.)

On the night of the third day, take it outdoors and bury it.

Knitted Binding

When someone repeated engages in harmful or disruptive behaviour, take your knitting needles and a length of black yarn. Cast on nine stitches, and then as you begin to knit the first row after casting on, for each stitch, focus on one particular behaviour or action they have done, and to yourself (or aloud) state, "[Name], you will never again disrupt or harm."

Repeat this for all nine stitches, and then do six more rows, repeating the same thing. As you cast off, on each cast-off stitch, state,

"I   bind   you   now   from   doing   harm,

to yourself, and others, now safe and warm."

This creates an energetic bookmark, which can be kept somewhere as a reminder, buried in your yard, or burned in a fire pit, as the binding is already accomplished fact.

To Bind Anger

Ingredients:

- Sand or sandy dirt

- Sea Salt

Mix the sand and salt, go outside, and take some in your right hand, saying:

Anger bound within my hand,

I cast you now back to the land.

With harm to none, and agendas stall,

replaced with peace and calm for all.

Throw the sand and salt over your left shoulder and return to your home without looking back.

CHAPTER SEVEN

Cleansing as Ritual and Preparation

Cleansing is an important aspect of all spellcraft, because it's the method we use to remove residual energy, fear, anger and doubt from our bodies, surroundings, and thoughts, in order to approach our work with the right awareness.

It's the means by which we remind ourselves who we really are at our sacred centre, and remove curses, spiritual attachments, and chaotic data from our experience and our minds.

We also use cleansing on the tools we will use for our working, and on the workspace itself.

Essentially, the only things we need not cleanse are the plants, flowers, herbs and roots with which we work, and any gold, iron or silver implements that have strictly been used by us alone. *(Any implements that have been shared by others should be ritually cleansed of any spiritual residue, intentional or unintentional, which may have been left behind by others.)*

Ritual Cleansing Baths

Cleansing baths are ancient rituals performed by followers of many traditions, and represent a restorative and efficient way to banish negative energy from your life.

In the Old Religions, they were an essential part of preparing for liturgical rituals as they can cleanse the mind, body and spirit for religious devotion as well.

Within our tradition, they are also useful precautions to "uncross" any hexes or obstacles that have been cast toward us, while allowing us the time to relax into our innate personal power.

Afro-Sicilian Cleansing Bath

Ingredients:

- Dried rue

- Dried calendula

- Epsom salts

- Lilac buds

- Blue lotus flower

- Lemon or Bergamot (fresh squeezed or essential oil)

- Sandalwood oil

Steps to Perform a Cleansing Bath

Fill your bath with warm (comfortable) water and add your aromatics and salts. Add a charcoal disc to your cauldron, or turn on an electric resin burner (making sure to keep it far enough away from water) and add a suitable resin incense blend (I prefer and recommend 1 part frankincense to one part Persian Sandarac). Don't add too much and make sure the room has some ventilation, as combined with imbued steam you can become overwhelmed.

I like the ambiance of a candle-lit room, but that is purely for aesthetic. Surround the bath with meaningful symbols, ritual tools, images and flowers.

Allow yourself to soak in the waters for 15 minutes, while declaring your intention to be ritually cleansed of any residual energies, hexes, curses, fears, doubt and anger -- body, mind and spirit.

When your bath is done, cup your hands around the resin burner, allowing the smoke to rise up between them, and feel/visualise the smoke being the final cleanse.

Weekly Cleanse

Once each week, on Saturday mornings, we would place some Persian Sandarac on the resin burner (or charcoal), and then hold a lemon over one another's head (one lemon for each person) for about 3-4 minutes. Then everyone together would hold the lemons over the sandarac smoke rising, and the lemons would be burned in a fire pit. This combines the Jupiter and Lunar energies to enhance our working for another week.

Intensive Cleanse

If an intense or important working was to be done on that Saturday, a small wisk, made from branches of rue, rosemary and basilico would be bound with a red ribbon or red twine, and the elder would "sweep" us from head to toe after the lemon cleanse, on the final step, using the wisk as an asperger, and "sprinkling" us with holy water and sea salt.

Strega Cleansing and Purifying Ritual Oil

Olio sacro della Santa Streghe (Chrism of the Holy Streghe) or Strega Oil is generally used for dispelling negative energy and to create boundaries against enemies. Protection, 'Piercing' or Averting the Evil Eye (*il malocchio*). This blend and combination of herbs and plants used is useful for both Offensive and Defensive Magic spell-work -- and is a suitable offering for Hecate/Hekate.

Uses : Protection, Hex Breaking, Banishing, Binding Spells, Cleansing Scrying Mirrors, Waning Moon, and New Beginnings.

Making the *Oil of the Sacred Streghe*

Principle Ingredients are rue and olive oil. This is why:

Rue (*Ruta graveolens*) is used in healing incenses and healing poppets; add to a bath to break all hexes and spells that may have been cast against you; and it is protective when hung up at the door in sachets. Rue's round-lobed leaves are said to have inspired the symbol for the suit of clubs.

Planetary association: Saturn | Elemental Association: Fire | Zodiac Association: Leo | Deity Association: Hecate, Diana - Magical uses of Rue include : Protection against the Evil Eye, healing, health, mental powers, and freedom. Sometimes used as an asperger to cast salt water for purification of the circle. Use for anointing magical objects, blessings, or in ritual. Holistically, Rue oil is used to ease the pain of arthritis, headaches, and general aches and pains. It is anti-inflammatory, antiviral, and antibacterial.

Olive oil is a traditional anointing oil used to aid in healing. Drawing a star with olive oil on the front door of a house is a common home blessing. This act can be part of a larger ritual.

Full Ingredients:

These are generally foraged or taken from the strega's own personal stores of the plants and herbs. The amounts are never measured.

- thyme (honours the ancestors),

- lotus flower (reincarnation or resurrection),

- lotus leaves,

- rue,

- holy basil (drives out negative energy and attracts prosperity),

- rosemary (cleansing, protection, blessing of pure memories),

- marjoram (happiness),

- sweetgrass (cleansing),

- sage (purification),

- agrimony (hex-breaking, reversal of spells, restful sleep),

- hyssop (consecration) and

- the smoke of Three Kings Incense, cedarwood, patchouli, and myrhh.

- The base is olive oil and Appalachian moonshine.

Steep the plants in a cup and a half of moonshine or Italian anisette for 3 days. On the fourth day, heat the mixture until half of the alcohol has evaporated. Add into the mixture a full cup of extra virgin olive oil.

You should begin the process of making the oil within days after the Full Moon, and allow it to bathe in moonlight until just after the New Moon.

In our tradition, the larger batches of this oil are made twice a year — once before the August Full Moon, and once around the time of *Luperca'lia* in February, again beginning within days of the February Full Moon.

Cleansing with Herbal Incense/Smudging

In addition to spells, there are herbs we can use to cleanse specific conditions:

- Lavender is burned to restore peace and relaxation.

- Rosemary is burned to promote peace and restore memory.

- Mugwort is burned to cleanse blockages to our intuition.

- Cedarwood is burned to protect and ground us.

- Juniper is burned to cleanse obstacles to prosperity and success.

- Thyme is burned to remove obstacles, mental blockages and negativity overall.

CHAPTER EIGHT

Divination in Southern Italy and Sicily

Divination -- the act of foretelling by supernatural or magical means the future, or discovering what is hidden or obscured -- derives from the Latin *divinationem*, which referred to the act of predicting or foreseeing "with the eyes (insight) of a deity".

Scopa Cards

In the Sicilian and Southern Italian traditions, one of the most popular means of divination was through the use of a *Scopa* deck -- a deck consisting of forty cards, four suits: *Denari* (coins), *Bastoni* (clubs), *Swords* (spades) and *Coppe* (cups). The cards range from the Ace to seven in each suit, with the court cards of *Fante* (knave), *Cavallo* (knight), and *Re* (king).

For every day readings, a three card spread would be normal. I normally use a modified spread, consisting of four cards. And for intensive readings, I use a nine-card spread.

A simple way to use the Scopa cards would be to ask a direct question. For example, one friend stopped by about six months ago, and said, "You know I wish I knew whether or not I should go with my instincts on this, but I am feeling very strongly like it's time to leave my job as a teacher, and do something completely different."

I offered to do a Scopa reading for her, and she agreed.

Now the first thing you always want to do when getting a reading is to make sure there is an energy exchange, as with any spellwork. So my friend reached into her purse, and pulled out a $20 bill and slapped it on the table.

These were the cards we pulled:

Fante di Denari (Paige of Coins) + 3 di Coppe (3 of Cups) + 7 di Coppe (7 of Cups)

This was interpreted as follows, first by looking at the raw meaning of each card:

- Fante di Denari - A female co-worker or close friend

- 3 di Coppe - New beginnings, early stages, immature

- 7 di Coppe - Intuition, wishes, inner self

Next came tuning into the whispers of the ancestors, which is a critical part of my readings, so that I can more accurately interpret what I am seeing. And from this, we derived the following interpretation:

There is a female co-worker and/or friend, whom you trust and have talked with about this. The idea itself is strong, and your intuition is correct, but right now the idea is in its infancy stages. So work on it, begin to develop it, and just don't jump the gun. If you and your friend continue to set the foundation, when it's firm and ready, you'll know when the right time is to launch.

Last week, after having taken my advice six months ago, my friend, who had indeed been working with two co-workers on starting a women's collective and art gallery idea, announced that she was leaving her job, and opening her gallery.

You can get a nice *Scopa* card deck here: https://amzn.to/3sYPzB2

Scopa Card Meanings

Understanding the cards comes with time, but the following can serve as a guideline from which to begin:

The Suits

- Spade (Spades or Swords) refer to problems, obstacles, pains and emotional hardships.

- Denari (Pentacles or Coins) refer to money, career, contracts, partnerships

- Coppe (Cups/Hearts) relate to love, family, affection and passion

- Bastoni (Clubs or Wands) represent goals, decisions, communications, social interaction and friends

Spade

Asso (Ace)- The ace of spades, perhaps the most famous card of ill omen, in a reading this indicates literal or metaphorical death, destruction, failure and ruin. Other meanings include protection, strength, significant, pay attention, important, warning

2- arguments, misunderstandings, conflict, separation

3- cheating, meddling, 3rd party influence, betrayal

4- inactivity, a halt, waiting, no action, illness

5- loss, endings, changes causing tears, rupture, cutting, break-ups, mishaps, accidents

6- obstacles, blocks, restrictions, external

influences, hinderance, inability to move forward, regrets, living in the past, emotional baggage

7- depression, sadness, suffering, grief, great problems, burdens, pain, uncertainty, clouded thinking, alcohol + drugs

Fante/Donna (Woman)- gossip, lies, a female enemy/rival, ex-wife/gf

Cavallo (Knave)- a man who is cunning, only cares about himself, can't be trusted, enemy, false person

Re (King)- authority, man in uniform, gov't official, police, doctor, ex hubby/bf, the Law

Denari

Asso- money, finances, wealth, business, commerce, shopping

2- unions, contracts, partnerships, marriage

3- little by little, increase, growth, branching out

4- letter, written communication, paperwork, faxes, documents, paper, information, messages

5- good luck, opportunity, chance, on the upswing , wheel of fortune, positive energy, attraction, Law of Attraction, accolades, recognition,

6- gifts, assistance, help, support

7-YES, success, realization of goals/wishes, abundance, achievement, dreams come true

Fante- female friend/acquaintance, coworker,

in-law

Cavallo- news, delivery man, the post, visitor

Re- male friend/acquaintance, coworker, boss, in-law

Coppe

Asso- love, heart, happiness, affection, sentiments, passion, fondness, pleasure

2- couple, relationship, mutual compatibility, harmony

3- child, new beginnings, small, innocence, early stages, youth, immature

4- home, house, family, domestic environment

5- improvements, positive changes, transitions, pregnancy, birth

6- the past, memories, healing, forgiveness

7- emotions, intuition, feelings, true love, inner self, wishes

Fante- sister, mother, female relative, dear friend

Cavallo- friend, faithful, loyal, supportive person/situation, sincerity

Re- father, brother, male relative, dear friend; however, this card is also an omen of self-sabbotage or self-destruction.

Bastoni

Asso- work, job, effort, will

2- crossroad, indecision, options, double

3- meetings, verbal communication, conversations, speaking, phone calls, chatting, discussions

4- security, stability, reliability

5- health, well-being, energy levels

6- gatherings, events, outdoors, parties, groups, socializing

7- studies, education, knowledge, facts, the mind

Fante- female significator, friend, lover, coworker

Cavallo- travel, trip, vacation, movement

Re- male significator, lover, friend, colleague

Tea Leaves, Coffee Grounds and Fava Beans

Another popular means of reading or divination were both coffee or tea leaf readings (examining the grounds/remains in a cup), as well as fava bean readings.

There could be an entire book devoted to the different ways in which different families in our region would actually perform this sort of divination.

Those who were said to have been marked with a particular birthmark were thought to be *prodigia* -- literally prodigies, who were marked with a sacred seal to represent the imprint of Source upon them as those able to see with the eyes of the divine.

The spells in this section are useful in seeking to strengthen your innate psychic abilities and divination skills.

Calling Forth Your Power

On a white round plate, arrange the following:

White candle, dressed with a drop of Strega Oil, some cinnamon, agrimony and lilac. You may wish to place a yellow obsidian crystal nearby, if you are certain that it is indeed obsidian, and not the more common faked pieces of yellow glass. You will also need a purple piece of yarn or thread.

Spell:

After lighting your candle, and centering your energy in alliance with whichever spiritual allies call out to you, if any, quietly speak your truth to power:

Psychic insight I now cast

for visions of future, present and past.

Open now the psychic eye

for divination and to scry.

Still the noise so I can hear

those with messages who draw near.

Unbind my spirit and free my mind,

and senses now no longer confined

to the worlds both seen and unseen be

open, aware and clear and free.

And so I cast, my will be done,

released to spirit,

manifest in ONE.

Next, taking the purple yard or thread, either cut it into three equal pieces and braid it, making nine or eighteen "crossings" or "ties"; or knot it into nine knots (like a witch's ladder); or knit it into eighteen knit stitches. Place the cord somewhere hidden from others, where you can see or hold it at times you want to call forth your powers.

Awareness Spell

On a plate, arrange a purple candle or votive, sprinkle around the candle, dried cinnamon, frankincense, basil, mugwort, wormwood and rue.

Sit quietly and lighting the candle, call on the energy of the Mother Earth - Gaia:

Mother Gaia -

Enlighten what's dark within and without;

Strengthen what's weak, within and without;

Mend what is broken, within and without;

Let me eyes be opened,

Let my heart be opened,

Let my ears be opened.

Increase in me the gifts of the psychic healer and seer.

As I speak this, so it is done.

Hold that space for at least thirty minutes, allowing the thoughts and images that arise to be gifted with your awareness.

Notice a subtle shift as the thoughts move from cursory thoughts or images to more meaningful ones.

Affirmations

In what I believe to be one of the finest and most lucid works on psychic magic of the 21st century, author and practitioner, Mat Auryn writes of the use of affirmations in a way that deeply resonated with my lived experience.

In the Italian and Afro-Sicilian tradition, we recognise that our life and our spiritual workings are on-going and constant, and that the purpose of our work is to become more mindful in the mundane, so that we're eventually aware that every thought and action is the creation of magic.

In his book, "*The Psychic Witch*[8]", Mat Auryn writes:

"As psychic witches, we understand the power of the spoken word and the power of thoughts. We understand that the internal world and external world are intricately linked. We know it's important that we take control of our own minds and energy, so that we can step into our personal sovereignty...

If a certain way of thinking is repeated, consciously or unconsciously, those pathways become the predominant ones used, leading to thinking or feeling in this manner more and more. This is called neuroplasticity. Now energetically the same is true. Energy pathways that are used

---

[8]   The Psychic Witch, Mat Auryn - Llewellyn Press, 2020 (https://amzn.to/3z0AGlD)

more become strengthened and easier to access,
while those that are ignored become weakened."

Within the remarkable exercises in Auryn's book are
mindfulness exercises, rituals, spells and illustrations that will
unquestionably do more to unlock your psychic potential than
anything I've seen done in any tradition, in more than a half-
century of practice. So please take the time to get that book, if
cultivating your psychic insight is important to you.

CHAPTER NINE

Dream Work & Entheogenic Journeying

Dating back to prehistoric times, medicine workers, mystics, shamanic practitioners and tribal elders have worked with their own dreams and those reported by members of the tribe as portals of consciousness, which inform us and allow us to explore other dimensions of being. Dreams are considered the portal through which the practitioners gain access to unconscious and even superconscious impulses and information not readily accessible in the waking state.

Entheogens -- a term derived from the Ancient Greek words ἔνθεος (*éntheos*) meaning "the indwelling divine", and γενέσθαι (*génesthai*) meaning "to generate", thus literally translating as *"becoming the divine within"* — are a family of psychoactive substances of plant origin, that are used in religious, ritual, or spiritual contexts. Jonathan Ott is credited with coining the term in 1979.

Entheogenic medicine has been part of the Afro-Sicilian and Italian esoteric traditions for millennia. Long understood for their ability to restore mental homeostasis at lower doses, it was also the foundation of sacred medicines that allow us to connect more deeply with the ancestors and Source on a fourth dimensional level, often understood as existing outside of the three-dimensional constructs of time and space.

In recent years, science has studied and validated the positive impact this sacred medicine can have on people suffering from mental health issues, as well as those struggling with life-threatening dis-ease.

It's use as a sacrament in the Mystery Traditions, including (as many now suspect) the possibility of it being at the foundation of the pre-institutional Christian mysteries, is recognised as the "magical bridge" between the mundane and ethereal levels of consciousness.

Modern examples of traditional entheogens include psychedelics, such as peyote, psilocybin mushrooms, ayahuasca, and iboga; atypical hallucinogens like *salvia divinorem*; quasi-psychedelics like cannabis; and deliriants like datura. These plants often include scientifically-identified compounds with psychoactive properties, or synthesised chemically. The organic and naturally-occurring compounds include mescaline, psilocybin, DMT, salvinorin A, ibogaine, ergine, and muscimol.

In 1962, an experiment was conducted on the day observed as Good Friday in Western Christianity, at Boston University. The experiment was conducted by Harvard Divinity School graduate, Walter Pahnke (under the guidance of Timothy Leary and Ram Das), and has come to be known as the Marsh Chapel Experiment (sometimes called the Good Friday Experiment).

Pahnke's experiment investigated whether psilocybin (the active principle in psilocybin mushrooms) would act as a reliable entheogen in religiously predisposed subjects.

Prior to the Good Friday service, twenty graduate degree divinity student volunteers were randomly divided into two groups. In a double-blind experiment, half of the students received psilocybin, while a control group received a large dose of niacin as a placebo.

Almost all of the members of the experimental group who received the entheogens reported experiencing profound religious experiences, providing empirical support for the theory that psychedelic drugs can facilitate spiritual experiences. One of the participants in the experiment was religious scholar Huston Smith, who would become an author of several textbooks on comparative religion. He later described his experience as "the most powerful cosmic homecoming I have ever experienced."

Thus, it's been common among the esoteric and mystical practitioners of our tradition to incorporate the use of the plant allies that fall into this category of "dreamweavers" and "mind expanders" into our spiritual work. Our practice honours the earth and everything connected to the earth. It acknowledges the magic and mystery of life and the spirit of everything around us.

For modern practitioners, interested in learning more about the use of baneful plants, medicinal nightshades and ritual entheogens, I would highly recommend Coby Michael's book, *The Poison Path*[9]. It's one of the best resources on the subject that I've seen in recent years.

Growing up in our tradition, much of the work that we did with entheogens, baneful plant allies and nightshades evolved as we grew older. Most of the elders in our family were inexperienced with most entheogens. The few who were happened to be very selective about those around whom they would speak of their experiences. But the references to "*il sentiero avvelenato*" (literally, *the poisoned path*) did frequently arise, and as a curious teen, this naturally led to discussions both within and outside the family, which would also result in experimentation with psychadelics. Not all of this experimentation was necessarily focused on the esoteric, but even those that were not were interpreted through the lens of our magical worldview, and therefore became part of my practice.

The spiritual, magical, and medicinal practices using these timeless plants and fungi as spiritual allies and aids can be found in the Mystery Schools of the Ancient world, both pre-dating and including the early proto-Catholic mysteries.

In the years of my seminary formation, I would learn more about the connections between the ancient Greek and Roman mystery schools, and the integration of their Great Sacrament into what would become the early Catholic liturgical practice and mystagogy.

---

[9] The Poison Path, Coby Michael (Park Street Press, 2021) https://amzn.to/3PHpws1

This "awakening" of one's innate magical power likely served as the inspiration behind some fanciful assertions made in the fourteenth and fifteenth century, including Johannes Hartlieb's claim[10] that the *"unholden"* (a Middle English term used to describe those who were not beholden to the abuses of the Christian religious patriarchy — i.e., freethinkers) would gather seven different baneful herbs — one on each day of the week — to create a *"witches' flying ointment"*.

These plants: borage, honesty, vervain, spurge, vetch, maidenhair fern and nightshade or datura, when combined, would have a mild to moderate entheogenic (or at least hallucinogenic) effect, which might have resulted in practitioners claiming to fly; although I doubt that its use was even certain. (Hartlieb omits the seventh herd, alleged to have been picked on Saturday, but experts often assert that it would be a nightshade or similar entheogen.)

The point being that there have been stories of magical practitioners, mystics and spiritual seekers using entheogens for millennia, as a means of discovering hidden mysteries.

And so, I came to understand the use of these entheogens as serving the purpose of "unlocking our spiritual DNA" -- enabling us to step into our power. This happens through the experiences of realisation that arise through the dreamwork and cultivation of a deeper relationship with these ancient plant and fungal allies.

The only variable was whether, when and how you chose to deal with that realization, and when and how you activated any or all of the attending powers.

Brother-witch, psychic, teacher and author, Mat Auryn posted a thoughtful and prosaic piece on *Patheos* entitled, *"You Cannot Be Taught to be a Witch"*, and as one might expect, it was met with some mixed emotions.

---

10   The Book of Forbidden Arts, Medieval Superstition and Magic, Johannes Hartlieb (1475) https://amzn.to/3NiXaTj

In no small part, from my perspective, many of those mixed emotions came from those who had decided in advance where they stood on the matter, before reading a word past the title. For others, a bit of defensive posturing seemed to arise out of their own experiences of marginalisation in pagan circles.

Here's an excerpt from Mat's article:

You can be taught witchcraft, but you cannot be taught to be a witch. This may seem like an odd statement from someone who teaches witchcraft for a living and has written a forthcoming book on witchcraft, but it's the truth.

I can no more teach you how to become a witch than I can teach a seed to sprout and grow. I can place the seed in the proper environment, water it, expose it to the right amount of sunshine and shade – but I cannot teach it to grow and transform into a plant. It must discover its own magick to do that on its own.

You cannot be taught to be a witch, but you can learn to be a witch. I can show you which words to recite out loud, when to whisper them and when to roar them.

I can show you which words to coat in honey and which to drench in vinegar as they come out of your mouth to paint the air, but I cannot teach you what honey or vinegar is to your soul. I can share with you a mystery but I cannot tumble it like amethyst within your mind until its smooth as glass and fits within your own palm.

I can hand you a crystal and show you how to hold it and which colored light in your Witch Eye to envelop it within, but I cannot make it sing for you nor can I make you hear its song.

I can show you the techniques to get into a trance state, where inner wells of power hide, what the different parts of your souls are. But I cannot teach you to truly seek, to tap into, to connect, to merge, and to integrate.

Only you can do this.

I can show you the process of examination and methods of deep inner healing, but I cannot teach you where those wounded aspects of yourself you keep under lock and key are concealed, especially those aspects you hide even from yourself. I can show you what to imagine and what to feel, but I cannot make you do either...

I can share with you my knowledge, my experiences, my thoughts, my musings. I can share with you the knowledge and experience of peers, students, and elders I've come to know either in person or from their written works.

I can never teach you how to understand that knowledge or enliven it as wisdom for you, despite however much I wish that I could.

I can show you how I cast spells, I can't get them to work for you. I can show you how to fly without your body, but I cannot lift you out of your body into the astral. I can show you how to call to gods and spirits, I cannot make them listen or respond to you.

I can teach you enchantments, I cannot enchant your own world for you. This is because being a witch is about power. It's the power of your soul and how it interacts with the ensouled universe that surrounds us.

We all have an individual relationship with the Witch Power that must be sought out on our own to be discovered...

Anyone can call themselves a witch. Anyone can take up the practice of witchcraft but not everyone who does so will truly become a witch. Despite this, anyone and everyone has the ability to be a witch...

I cannot navigate the blessings and the curses that the Witch Power will throw upon your crooked path to cocoon you for your transmutation.

The words of the Star Goddess weave throughout all things, threading together the currents of power that calls to the soul of the witch. Like a sphinx she riddles the mystery, supplying both lock and key to those people who would transform themselves into witches as caterpillars metamorphose into moths, compelled to the moon's light with unstoppable drive – a riddle that is different for every single witch.

"And thou who thinkest to seek for me, know

thy seeking and yearning shall avail thee not,

unless thou know this mystery: that if that which

thou seekest thou findest not within thee, thou

wilt never find it without thee."

– Charge of the Goddess (Auryn, 2019)

Naturally, it's not my intention to recommend the use of any plant etheogens or even to suggest that you apply anything shared within this book, outside of offering an educational and informative look into my personal practice. But I do think it's worth underscoring what Mat Auryn points out in his article — that the journey you take, and the identities that arise from them, are entirely yours to make.

The spells and exercises I offer in this chapter are designed to encourage and foster a deeper relationship with some of the entheogens, nightshades and baneful plants with whom I have cultivated a personal relationship over the past half-century of practice.

If they inspire you to explore that possibility, then I wish you nothing but joyful discovery!

"The Poison Path is a spiritually based practice that explores the esoteric properties of potentially deadly plants, and while many of them have entheogenic qualities, it was their poisonous nature that first attracted me... While the study of ritual entheogens can keep one busy for decades, we should not assume that they are the only way of accessing certain states of consciousness. It is a subcategory or supplemental set of tools and knowledge that can be utilized to enhance one's spiritual tradition... The plants that belong to the Poison Path are among many guides and allies that we will meet along the way."

Coby Michael - author of The Poison Path

Entheogenic Spellcraft

Unguento da Sogno Cosmico (Cosmic Dreamwork Salve)*

The nearest formula to a "witches flying ointment" I've found mentioned in all of the family formularies and traditions handed down to me from the earliest days of the Common Era would be the one for our *Unguento da Sogno Cosmico*. And it's one that has frequently been a popular, if not best-seller, when I had my shops.

Ingredients:

- 2 oz vodka or grain alcohol

- 1 cup olive oil

- 13 tablespoons of beeswax

- 1 oz. Atropa belladonna (belldonna)

- 1/2 oz Artemesia vulgaris (mugwort)

- 1/4 oz Psychotria viridis (chacruna)

- 1/4 oz ruta graveolens (Italian rue)

- 8 drops of oudh oil

- Essential oil of red rose (10 drops)

- Essential oil of frankincense (10 drops)

- Essential oil of sandalwood (10 drops)

- Essential oil of rosemary (10 drops)

Preparation:

1. In a sealed jar, soak belladonna, mugwort, chacruna and rue in 1/4 oz of vodka or grain alcohol for 15 days, beginning on a Full Moon.

2. Strain through cheesecloth, and place plant materia in a clean, fire-safe bowl or cauldron. Taking proper safety precautions, when the plant materia has dried, burn it on a Saturday evening. Reserve 1/4 tsp of the ash, and add it to the olive oil.

3. While the plant materia is steeping in the alcohol, take a separate mason jar, and add the olive oil (with ash), the rue, oudh, rose, frankincense, sandalwood and rosemary oils, and reseal the jar, allowing to sit in a cool, dark cabinet.

4. On the New Moon, take the strained alcohol tincture, and add to the mason jar of oil, and simmer (placing it into a sauce pan filled half-way with water, so that the jar is warmed, but does not "float") over low-heat for six hours. Increase the heat (adding more hot water, if necessary) and

slowly pour in 13 tablespoons of beeswax, stirring until the entire mixture is well blended.

5.   Pour into two 4-ounce tins, seal. And allow to sit on a window sill or ledge under the waxing moon until the next Full Moon.

This ointment or salve is best used on an empty stomach, after a cleansing bath, at a time when the practitioner can sit or lay down undisturbed for a period of four to six hours. Dreamwork music or binaural beats are often reported to be helpful in achieving the quieted state of mind, necessary for cosmic insight and journey work.

The Sacramental Journey

It's difficult to ascertain from the stories handed down to me whether this particular tradition actually evolved out of the Catholic Conjure side of our practice, or whether its inclusion in Catholic Conjure was simply a modernisation of our family traditions related to the ancient mystery traditions.

But that there is a specific elixir that shows up in various stories handed-down to me and my family, both with relationship to the ancient mysteries, and the role our family played in crafting these entheogenic wines, as well as purported roles that we played in providing "sacred wine" to a select and secretive sect within the Catholic Church.

As a skeptic, I take such stories with a grain of salt, realising that the true stories are likely heavily embellished over the centuries; but it was striking to me that something I almost dismissed as being mostly embellishment has begun to be uncovered by scholars, studying the enthogenic and psychedelic "sacraments" in both the mystery traditions and in the paleo-Christian movement (which I call the proto-catholic tradition).

In his book, *The Immortality Key*[11], author Brian Muraresku asks provocative questions that explore the possible connections between the Dionysian Mysteries and the Jesus Mysteries, and dig into the archaeological and DNA evidence that suggests psychedelics played an important role in mystagogy, possibly within all of the ancient mystery school traditions.

This is the elixir or sacred wine formula that has been used for cultivating profound connections with our Ancestors, the Divine Source Within, and which those of us who have partaken of it, almost unanimously report as having transformed and healed our lives in ways that I can barely begin to express (speaking from personal experience of it).

Il Sacro Elisir dei Mistagoghi (Sacred Elixir of the Mystagogues)*

This formula during a period of sacred festival, ranging from the last day of October through the 6th day of November, encompassing the sacred feasts honouring the Great Ancestors, Proserpina and Her Mother (Demeter), the Feasts of All Saints and All Souls, and the Festival of Shadows.

Ingredients:

- 60 grams dried *Amanita muscaria* (mushrooms)
- 1 pomegranate (seeds crushed to pulp)
- 3 tsp lemon juice
- 1 litre of an acidic wine, made from the Piedirosso grape, such as *Lacryma Christi del Vesuvio* (Christ's Tears for Vesuvio)

---

[11] The Immortality Key: The Secret History of the Religion with No Name, Brian Muraresku, St. Martin's Press (2020) https://amzn.to/3MhSSub

Preparation:

1. In a medium saucepan, add 1/3 litre of wine, amanita, pomegranate, and lemon juice. Heat on simmer for 4 hours. If necessary, add a small amount of hot water to keep liquid from cooking off.

2. Strain through cheesecloth, and allow to cool completely. Add into a clean decanter, and pour in the other 2/3 of the wine.

3. Serves 10 for mild entheogenic experience, or four for deep entheogenic experience. Take with bread to avoid stomach upset.

4. Can be bottled into dark blue medicine decanters, and taken in 1 mg medicine dropper dosages for "microdosing".

"If these sacraments survived for thousands of years in our remote prehistory, from the Stone Age to the Ancient Greeks, did they also survive into the age of Jesus? Was the Eucharist of the earliest Christians, in fact, a psychedelic Eucharist?"

Brian Murareshu, author of The Immortality Key

*Reminder

The formulas provided in this book are offered for educational purposes only, and are not meant to diagnose, treat, or serve as prescriptions for any conditions. Implementation of this information for your personal use, while perfectly within your rights to do so, should be undertaken at your own risk. Neither the author nor the publisher is responsible for any adverse effects that come from your use of the information contained anywhere in this book.

Final Thoughts on the Entheogenic Path

For me, the value of integrative psychedelic medicine is that it allows us to move beyond the three competing notions (all three of which are delusional) in our society.

The first delusion imagines that what the primitive minded cultures (and those who still subscribe to primitive spiritual notions) call "god" is an all-powerful, judgmental and grotesquely manipulative Being outside of ourselves, requiring our absolute subservience in order to achieve an unnecessary "salvation" of some sort.

That group has murdered countless souls in defense of its indefensible religious superstitions.

The second delusion imagines that we ourselves are the Source Itself. By adopting the superstitious constructs of the first group, this group imagines that the purpose of life is to become "self-realised" and obtain apotheosis.

The danger of that delusion is that it ignores the ego and super-ego, and seldom takes into account the miracles and opportunities for miracles that exist all around them.

The third group suffers from a delusion of completely dry, listless secularism.

Disempowered like the first group, they often feel powerless to the whims of time and space, but without any hope for anything beyond this existence. And distracted by that secularism, they, like the second group, miss out on the miracles occurring all around them.

But there is a fourth group, which has existed on the fringes... living beyond the hedge of societal norms, who have experienced an Eternal Wisdom that offers few answers, but stimulates us to daily ask better questions. It allows them to see themselves as an inextricable part of the ALL, while realising that the identities with which we toy are but functions of what the Cosmos itself is doing.

And interestingly, it's not that the second group was wrong entirely, for we indeed are perfectly expressed avatars of the Ground of Being Itself. Where they get lost is in not realising that their gods and goddesses are not Source, but likewise are aspects or avatars of Source Itself. The only difference is that you and I are three-dimensional beings, and they are four-dimensional beings. So they can exist outside of time and space naturally, while we have yet to master that capability.

The work I do as an esoteric contemplative, serving as an alchemist and architect of solutions -- a *fattucchiero*, as my ancestors would call me -- is that the magic I work with... the very same power that is your birthright... I use with the intention of raising the consciousness of Source Expressing As Me, so that suffering and pain no longer exists for any sentient being. It's my choice. My way, if you will.

In that, I acknowledge something I read from one of my greatest mentors and influencers, as a young man. Alan Watts wrote, "Through our eyes, the universe is perceiving itself. Through our ears, the universe is listening to its harmonies. We are the witnesses through which the universe becomes conscious of its glory, of its magnificence." And upon reading those words, I understood why my ancestors did the esoteric and mystical work that we've done for centuries.

It was the moment I chose to pick up that mantle myself.

CHAPTER TEN

Financial Prosperity Spells

Prosperity spells can be used as a way to attract something that you want in your life. It is not just about getting what you want, but also about manifesting what you want in your life, and then attracting more of it.

A prosperity spell is a spell that brings about wealth, prosperity and good luck to the caster or the intended subject. Prosperity spells are often cast with the intention of bringing financial success and abundance into the caster's life. Prosperity spells can be cast for oneself or on behalf of another person.

Whether you're looking to stretch what feels like your last dollar or finally get that promotion (and pay raise) you deserve, prosperity spells include potions and incantations for financial and personal success.

Within the Afro-Sicilian tradition, prosperity also includes health and an abundance of the immaterial things that make us happy -- loving relationships, supportive family and friends, community and an easy road ahead.

The Coffee Spell

One of the simplest forms of abundance and prosperity spells I have ever done is one that became part of my daily routine.

I begin each day with ancestral work, which we've talked about. And that work always involves making an offering to the ancestors, which in the morning, is always a cup of coffee and some biscotti or sweets.

And because we want the afterlife to be sweet and prosperous for our ancestors, we incorporate this simple spell into each morning's ritual.

Ingredients:

- Coffee (brewed)

- Italian sweet cream

- Sugar (optional)

- Anisette (optional)

Preparation:

1. Pouring your coffee, say, "Brewed from the earth, gift of the land, this offering made from my heart and my hand. Sweetened with cream, stirred three times three, draw abundance and sweetness and prosperity."

2. Add the creamer and other sweeteners, and stir clockwise three times, thrice. (Total of nine revolutions in the cup with your spoon.)

3. I take one cup for the ancestors and place it before their pictures or on the ancestral altar, and one cup for me, and I sit with them to drink that first brew of the day. After 30 minutes, I thank them and the spirits of the house and land, and pour the coffee out into the garden as an offering to the earth itself.

Career Spell

If you wish to embark on a new career, do this spell on the Full Moon.

Ingredients:

- Green 7-Day Candle

- Grape leaves (6)

- A Pin or Scissors

Preparation:

Engrave upon the top of the candle a symbol, sigil or word that represents the job you are trying to secure. It can be as simple as the company name or logo.

Place the candle on a fire-safe plate, and arrange six grape leaves around the bottom of the candle.

Say the following words as you light the candle:

Bella Luna by this moon

Secure my job and bring it soon

Wealth and fortune, silver, gold,

all you send my hands can hold.

Let the candle burn for seven days, or until it goes out on its own. (Never blow the candle out, extinguish it with a candle snuffer, or a plate placed on top.)

Charm Bag

A small green pouch filled with the herb vervain, a penny, nickle, dime and quarter, secured with red or green thread, prepared during the waxing moon, and consecrated with the smoke of frankincense and copal, while speaking this spell:

The Bella Luna is a golden coin, which I carry

in my heart. It draws to me abundance, beauty,

prosperity and art.

Keep the charm bag in your left pocket or place it in a drawer, in the left corner of your house, beginning on the full moon.

Il Magico Incantesimo di Nonna Cafolla per Attirare l'Abbondanza

(Grandma Cafolla's spell for attracting abundance)

My great grandmother had a Full Moon prosperity spell that I saw her work for one of her daughters with great success. It's one of the oldest full spells I wrote in my childhood journals, after the Malocchio removal spell.

Ingredients:

- A shot glass filled with sugar and cinnamon (mixed)

- A traditional coffee cup and saucer

- A silver dollar or 1000 lire (£.1,000) coin

- A white candle with a green ribbon tied around it

Preparation:

- On a clean placemat at the kitchen table, where the Full Moon can be seen from a window or door, place the coffee cup and saucer on top of a silver dollar or £.1,000 piece.

- Insert the shot glass, filled with the cinnamon-sugar mix.

- Carefully add enough water to the coffee cup to come up to about 1/3 of the outside of the shot glass, being careful not to get the cinnamon-sugar wet.

- Light the candle and focus your energy on how the fire reflects the energy of that fire within, and recall that ours were the ancestors of Moon and Water.

- Incantation over the cup, charging it with your power:

Lucifera, la Bella Luna
Mentre la tua luce si riflette sull'acqua
e la tua dolcezza rinvigorisce questa cannella e
zucchero,
attiro i doni dell'abbondanza e della prosperità
che sono il mio diritto di primogenitura come tuo
figlio.
Poiché non manchi mai di rispondere alla mia
chiamata,
non mancherò mai di onorare la tua bellezza e il
tuo mistero.

English:
Lucifera - La Bella Luna
As your light reflects off the water,
and your sweetness invigorates this cinnamon
and sugar,
I draw down the boons of abundance and
prosperity that are my birthright as your child.
Because you never fail to answer my call I will
never fail to honour your beauty and mystery.

- Allow the working to absorb the energy of the Full Moon and Water for three hours. Leave the candle to burn until it burns out on its own.

- After three hours, drink the water, setting the cinnamon-sugar aside somewhere safe.

- Each day for three days, start your day with a cup of black coffee, sweetened with the cinnamon sugar (and you can add Italian sweet cream, if you wish). Express your gratitude for the sweetness as a reminder of the abundance being drawn into your experience.

- Keep the coin in your pocket or purse as a curio or token amulet to continue to draw in that abundance.

CHAPTER ELEVEN

Healing Spells

For our ancient ancestors, magic gave people a means to attain what their hearts desired — protection, divination, healing, luck, vengeance and, most of all, a sense of empowerment. It has been called a measure of comfort in a cold, dark world.

But for our ancestors, there was an underlying sense that what we were doing, regardless of the road taken, was healing those who were suffering.

Those who needed protection were healed from oppression. Those who sought out our divination were healed from their fear and uncertainty. Those who sought our work for vengeance were healed from the injustices that were visited upon them.

We find many forms of healing magic in our tradition, from talismanic to elixirs and balms.

For the practitioner, we recognise the healing that we facilitate always begins within ourselves. We listen to the energy systems of our physical and astral bodies, and take actions to correct whatever it is that allows imbalance to occur in our own experiences. This, then sets the stage to create the causes and conditions for healing of those with whom we come in contact.

I always begin a spiritual session, counseling. or magical working with a client by sharing with my private clients what I believe. The purpose is not to change what they think or believe, but so that they can understand the perspective from which my advice and counsel comes. From there, we can respectfully agree to disagree, if necessary, on any of the finer points.

That might seem surprising to many of you, because traditional counseling is approached from the perspective that I am going to teach you how to think and how to solve your problems.

That approach is completely unnecessary in my field of practice, because I don't recognise or concern myself with analysing what you are doing wrong. My only concern is in healing myself!

Let me explain. I believe that each of us is responsible for all our experiences without exception. Everything we encounter or experience in our "external world" is nothing more than a reflection of some thought, some belief, or "chaotic data" within my own subconscious mind.

Now you may be thinking that if each of us is responsible for our own experiences, then that means you are responsible for your experiences, and you are correct. But my encounter with you is my personal experience. And that encounter is reflecting something about my interior mindset -- in other words, it's like a CD that's been burned of the data that's on my subconscious mind's "hard drive". So what I have to work on is my own data, because when I clear that chaos and disinformation, my experiences will reflect balance, harmony and ease, and that will be reflected in the lives of everyone I encounter.

So these spells are generally done to bring about healing within, and as a result, without.

Simple Healing Spell

This spell can be worked for general healing in your life and the lives of those around you, or with specific intent.

Ingredients:

- One blue candle

- Six cloves

Preparation:

1. Dress the candle with six cloves (if working with a pillar candle, place them in a circle around the candle, or pierce

the candle, pushing them into the candle; when working with a glass votive candle, arrange them in a circle around the base of the candle, which should be placed on a fire-safe plate).

2. Charge the candle by drawing out the love and healing energy from your heart-centre and energising it, saying, "I consecrate and charge this candle as a physical tool for healing and representation of the healing that is already underway on the ethereal plane."

3. Next focus on healing rising up within you, touching every place in your life that there is pain or illness. Envision that healing spreading out from the top of your head to the area surrounding you, and then in ripples, generating wave-after-wave of healing that reaches everyone you know and don't know.

4. If there is a specific person for whom you are doing this working, picture them being enveloped in this wave of healing energy as well.

5. Say, "Magic mend and candle burn, sickness end, and health return."

6. Let the candle burn until it goes out on its own.

Healing Oil

*   4 drops Rosemary Oil

*   2 drops Juniper Oil

*   1 drop Sandlewood Oil

*   2 drops Lavender Oil

*   30 ml Camelia Oil

This oil can be carried or worn as a healing charm.

Strega Healing Balm

People who have known our family come to me year-after-year for this healing balm, which I usually make on Holy Saturday night, just as the sun sets.

Ingredients:

- 3/4 cup of Calendula Oil

- 1/4 cup of Coconut Oil (fractionated)

- 6 teaspoons beeswax

- 1/4 teaspoon Arrowroot

- 10 drops Lavender Oil

- 5 drops Rue oil

- 5 drops Rose oil

- 3 drops Oudh

Preparation:

1. Add water to a saucepan or double boiler.

2. Mix Calendula, coconut oil and beeswax, and stir until completely melted.

3. Add lavender, rue, rose and oudh, stirring well and remove from heat. Mix in arrowroot and stir. (You have to work quickly at this point)

4. Pour into tins or small glass jars, and allow to cool completely.

5. Once poured, place your hands over the tins or jars and say,

Through the Divine Essence, which is the breath
of life Itself, I charge and consecrate this balm
as a healing vehicle for all who wear it. So shall
it be.

The instructions I give to the person who will use it is to place it on or near the area that needs healing, saying:

Today I use this healing balm,
　　to boost my health and bring me calm.

CHAPTER TWLEVE

Knotwork & Knitting

As I've said throughout this book, our tradition has always seen little distinction between the acts of ritual magic and the magic performed in the mundane tasks of every day.

Believed to have originated in the Middle East in the 5th Century of the Common Era, knitting has been one of those things that seem to have been both magical and mundane from the start. Even the earliest records and stories of knitting speaks of blessings being woven into the pieces.

The word is derived from knot, thought to originate from the Dutch verb knutten, which is similar to the Old English *cnyttan*, "to knot".

Fishermen in Europe began to knit warmer textiles for wearing at sea, and their very nets can be seen, since ancient times as being a form of knitting.

Beyond the magical transformation that comes from quieting our minds, and learning patience -- two skills that organically arise from the act of knitting or crocheting -- there is an empowering aspect to knitting magic, which strengthens the practitioner's skills in general.

Undertaking a knitted spell, we may find a dropped stitch, or other mistake in our work, which then calls upon our creativity to make it right. This reminds us of our power to correct the things that need tweaking in our other workings.

Knitted magic connects us with the archetypes of Arachne and Aridane -- the mythological weavers of the ancient stories. We draw on that energy of Arachne when we need to draw out the truth in a situation, or on Aridane when we need to open the road in the labyrinth of life.

Knitting is also knotwork, and therefore it is a powerful means of warding someone or some place. The Celts, who once ruled Sicily, believed that knotwork was a means of manifestation -- a physical reminder of our dreamwork, and so we would see the knitted work as a means of connecting with our spiritual allies known as the linchetti (the dream weavers of our culture).

When someone is seriously ill, I will often knit a bookmark or coaster for them, often from a precious textile or yarn, repeating a healing spell on each stitch, as a means of giving them a "touchstone" for the magic I've done and released into the universe.

A witch's ladder (also known as "rope and feathers", witches' ladder, witches' ladder, or witch ladder) is a practice, in folk magic or witchcraft, that is made from knotted cord or hair, that normally constitutes a spell. Charms are knotted or braided with specific magical intention into the cords.

Knot spells are one of the most primordial types of magic known to man, common across almost all cultures and traditions. There's a Babylonian tablet in the British museum detailing a healing spell involving knots plaited in cedar bark, while Roman author, Pliny the Elder, claimed that wounds healed more quickly if bound with the Hercules knot.

But even if you are a novice or don't know how to knit at all, you can do the following spells simply by making knots in a cord or piece of yarn; however, there is just something about picking up a pair of bamboo or steel knitting needles, and knowing that you're creating something with these ancient tools.

Practical Applications

When reciting any spell, you can enrich or increase its impact by "knitting" the spell into a textile. Each stitch becomes a "knot" that represents the unbreakable bond of the outcome to bend to your will.

So, if you were doing a spell for protection, for example, you could easily repeat a simple declaration of protection, "With each stitch protect and safeguard (Name) from harm or foul." (Do six stitches — all knit stitches, and twelve rows or 15 rows, and you will have a nice little book mark. Give it as a gift with a book to the person you are protecting.)

An alternative is to do a "protect and bind" piece in which you knit one row, and pearl the next. On the knit row, do as stated above, but on the pearl rows, state what you want to bind. I'll give an example:

Let's say your sister is dating a guy you don't trust, because you know his mother is a meddling pain in the ass. You light your candle to focus your energy, and then sit down to knit. I would recommend using red yarn (see the colour correspondences below) for protection.

On the knit stitches, you say, "Protect and ward my sister from harm or foul." And on the pearl stitches, "Keep his mother away from meddling now."

So your sister will be protected, and the mother's hands will be "bound" by each stitch to prevent her meddling.

Colour Correspondences for Yarn or Thread

Each colour has a specific properties associated with it. So we choose the colour that corresponds with the qualities we want to invoke.

- White – Spirituality, protection, and cleansing.

- Yellow – Communication, intellect, learning, concentration, action, and wisdom.

- Orange – Empathy, confidence, legal matter, and pride.

- Red – Ambition, vigor, endurance, passion, lust, and ambition.

- Pink – Friendship, gentleness, reconciliation, and love.

- Purple – The Divine Androgyne. Psychic matters, success, commitment, and power.

- Blue – Healing, guidance, spirituality, truth, and happiness.

- Green – Fertility, employment, good luck, prosperity, and beauty.

- Brown – Nature, grounding, the animal kingdom, security, and lost things.

- Grey – Divination, psychic awareness, legal matters, and secrets.

- Black – Rebirth, binding, stability, and divination.

- Silver – The Goddess/Divine Feminine, the Moon, visions, and intuition.

- Gold – The God/Divine Masculine, the Sun, life forces, and longevity.

CHAPTER THIRTEEN

Il Malocchio (Evil Eye)

Nazal is the name for the evil eye in Turkey, *Mal de Ojo* in Central America and Mexico, *Drishti* in India, *Zle Oko* in Poland, and within the Afro-Sicilian magical tradition, having spread to much of what is now considered to be Italy, we call it *malocchio*.

Within our culture, we believe that whenever someone looks at us with envy, jealousy, irritation or disdain, they impart *il malocchio* -- the evil eye. And this evil eye will bring misfortune, loss or illness.

The person giving you the look, as we often called it, doesn't even necessarily have to intend that misfortune befalls you.

Within the texts of ancient manuscripts from Greece, Rome and Persia, we see that there was a fascination with the power of the evil eye, which undoubtedly contributed to the beliefs that surround il malocchio in the Afro-Sicilian and Southern Italian traditions.

Even in the Jewish and Muslim spiritual texts, we read about the enchantments of the evil eye:

"I said to them, 'Cast away, each of you, the detestable things of his eyes, and do not defile yourselves with the idols of Egypt; I am the LORD your God.'" (Ezekiel 20:7)

"Say: 'I seek refuge with the Lord of the Dawn, from the mischief of created things; From the mischief of darkness as it overspreads; From the mischief of those who practice secret arts; and from the mischief of the envious one as he practices envy'." (Quran 113:1-5)

As far back as 3000 BCE, there are mentions of the evil eye in ancient Egyptian writings and so this is one of those traditions that illustrates how Sicilia was a melting pot of various cultures and traditions over the millennia.

It is said that malocchio can be given in four ways, including by malice, by *attaccatura* (attachment), by *fascino* (binding), or by *fattura* (fixing).

It is believed that the most common way to receive or give malocchio is by excessive compliments or praise, especially if the praise is much more than deserved.

This is why in Italy most compliments are followed by "*Sii benedetto*," literally, "Be blessed," to avoid giving any accidental malocchio.

The symptoms of malocchio include being the recipient of uncharacteristic bad luck, poor health, or accidental loss. Perhaps you could experience severe headaches, nausea, even a loss of strength. Or something that was going well, until someone heaped excessive praise on them or on it, will suddenly start to fall apart.

The belief that such an overlook can trigger such a turn of events even extends to the life of the expectant mother. If a pregnant person sees someone with a birth defect -- a large mole, or cleft palate, perhaps -- that pregnant person will immediately touch their butt, before touching anywhere else, especially the face, so that if malocchio was given, the defect will show up on the infant's butt, not their face or upper body.

The "diagnosis" of the malocchio varies widely from region to region, but generally states that even if you have a strike of bad luck you've been cursed. Lifting of this curse goes through few "treatments" performed by "healer", and these approaches vary from region to region as well.

Preventative protection includes the use of a "*portafortuna*" or good luck charm, worn around the neck, such as the Italian Horn (*cornicello* or *cornu*), the *manu figa*, or the hanging of a *cimaruta* (especially in children's rooms and in the family room or kitchen.

Cimaruta (Italian for 'sprig of rue') is an ancient Italian charm, worn around the neck, or hung above an infant's bed to ward off malocchio.

Based on the sacred rue herb, which has medicinal properties, and is also believed to protect against poisoning and sorcery. A Cimaruta is traditionally made of silver, with multiple different small charms branching off from the central stalk of the rue plant. The types of charms that hang from a specific cimaruta depend on the family, the region, and the intentions, such as symbols of strength, protection, power, fertility, health, healing and psychic warding.

In this section, we will give an overview of the two methods of diagnosing and removing malocchio, as shared publicly by other practitioners. In the interest of full disclosure, within my family's tradition, this is taught on Christmas Eve (after midnight Mass) when we are six years-old, and it is never taught publicly. So there are some differences in the way that I perform the diagnosis or removal; but I will not be sharing them in this book, out of respect for our family tradition.

We're fortunate to have other practitioners, whose family made no such obligations to secrecy necessary. And I can promise you that I have used each of the methods below, and they all work.

Diagnosing Malocchio

The ritual diagnostics to determine whether a person has been afflicted with *il malocchio* is done with the subject (the person suspected of having malocchio) seated at the kitchen table, with their hands in their lap, feet uncrossed, and flat on the floor.

Ingredients:

- A soup bowl (porcelain or ceramic, never metal)

- A bottle or pitcher of water

- A bottle of olive oil

- Scissors

- Blessed sea salt

Preparation:

1. Pour water into the soup bowl, about 3/4 of a serving. You want the bowl to be "full" but not so full that you cannot steadily hold it over the subject's head.

2. Slowly and deliberately place six drops of olive oil into the bowl, not too close together.

3. Carefully lift the bowl and place it on the top of the head of the subject (while still holding it of course). Try not to move it around too much.

4. Observe the oil - If the oil drops burst into many smaller droplets and spread out, unintentional malocchio is is present. If the drops all come together to form one giant drop, intentionally-thrown malocchio is present. If the drops remain relatively the same, no malocchio is present.

Removing (Breaking) the Malocchio

Place the bowl on the table, and if the malocchio is present, recite the *scongiuro* (conjuration) in Southern Italian dialectic.

Some of the cousins would say this little bit in English, which I suspect came from Zio Leo Martello's influence: "Powers of the north above, the south below, east and west to my side, before and behind me, protect me." Personally, I wasn't taught to do so, and have never done so.

Il Scongiuro

Recite this slowly and deliberately:

San Sisto, San Sisto,

Lo spirito tristo,

E mala morte,

Di giorno e notte,

Caccia da questa,

Caccia da noi,

Strappa e calpesta

Ogni occhio che nuoce,

Qui faccio la Croce.

(Translation into English)

San Sisto, San Sisto,

Throughout the day and night,

Drive away from this person and from us,

This dark spirit and miserable death.

Tear out and stomp upon every eye that seeks to

harm,

And here I make the sign of the Cross.

At the point that you say the words "*Qui faccio la Croce*," grab a pinch of the sea salt, and make a cross on the water, then pick up the scissors, and open them, and with one blade, cut through the oil three times. Holding the scissors above the bowl and cut the air three times, saying, "*Crepa l'occhio triste! Crepa l'occhio triste! Crepa l'occhio triste! Gia finuto.*" (The Evil Eye bursts! And so it is finished!)

On my grandmother's side of the family, the ritual was then over. On the Salvato side of the family, we would take a drop of olive oil on our thumb and make a cross on the top of the head, the third eye, and heart of the subject, and then wash our hands. The oil and water would be thrown out in the soil outside, or flushed down the toilet. If we threw it down the toilet, a pinch of the blessed salt was thrown in after you flushed.

CHAPTER FOURTEEN

Protection Spells

It's said that within the Afro-Sicilian and Southern Italian esoteric traditions, protection spells were among the oldest uses for magic our ancestors recorded and passed down to future generations.

Unlike the more complex magical systems we find in the ancient Egyptian, Greek and Roman worlds, our ways were often more practical and relied on items commonly on-hand, which could even be "hidden in plain sight" when necessary.

By working closely with the plant spirits as allies, we are able to protect ourselves spiritually and physically, since modern science has shown many of these plant allies contain phytochemicals or other compounds that literally help defend the body against bacterial and viral attacks.

Garlic, for example, contains components found to block covalent binding of carcinogens to DNA, enhance degradation of carcinogens, have anti-oxidative and antibacterial properties.

And so we'll begin with a simple, powerful and common protection spell, using a *"Treccia d'aglio"* (Garlic Braid).

Garlic Braids

It's association with Mars and the element of fire makes garlic a valuable spiritual ally in protecting, banishing and warding our homes.

A braid, made with six or nine heads of garlic, will prevent harmful energies, jealous people or those with hidden agendas from entering our homes.

Mixing dried garlic with sea salt, kept in a small pouch in one's apron or pocket was something the homemaker would do, when someone was coming they didn't trust. As the person left, this mixture would discreetly be sprinkled behind them, into their footsteps.

How to Braid Garlic

You'll need six or nine bulbs of garlic for this. First off, prepare your bulbs for planting by gently rubbing any big chunks of dirt from the outside layer, and trimming the roots short.

Tie the first three bulbs together as seen in the illustration, using kitchen twine.

Next, place a bulb right in the middle of your initial trio. Lay the stalk straight down the middle. Now, cross the right stalk over the top (again, just like normal braiding).

Select another bulb, and lay it on the right side. Lay the stalk so it's in the middle (the stalk of the newly added bulb will always go in the middle).

Cross the left-side stalks over the middle, just like normal braiding.

Now add a bulb to the left side of the bunch. Lay the stalk of this new bulb in the middle bunch, and cross the right side over. Once you've done that, add another bulb to the middle, and keep going until you're out of garlic.

When you're done adding bulbs to the braid, you'll have a handful of stalks. Continue to braid these in a simple braid until you reach the end. Tie tightly with another bit of string (I like to make a loop so I can easily hang the braid).

Store the garlic in a cool, dry place (avoid anywhere with lots of humidity, like a damp basement). Preferably, hang next to or above the door.

In our tradition, we use garlic to ward off hexes, curses, and the common cold. Whole garlic bulbs and cloves of garlic can be made into charms. Crushed, sliced, and minced garlic can be used in magical edibles, such as potions, soups, sauces, and roasts.

Used the dried powder in sachet bags, spell bottles, jar spells, and more.

There are two *scongiuri* (charms) that are incanted while braiding the garlic, depending on whether you're doing it to protect a person or to protect your whole home.

To protect a person:

Unpeeled layers of garlic skin
> shield with safety those within.
> Braided to keep harm at bay,
> Protect (Name) now, by night and day.

To protect the whole home or business:

Garlic wrapped around a braid,
> This *santuccio* I have made.
> Protect this place and all who visit
> from harm, disease, and what else is it.
> Baneful energy flee from me,
> as I have willed, so shall it be.

Other Protection Spells

Red Ribbon & Rue

A sprig of Italian rue (*ruta graveolens*) tied with a red ribbon or red yarn, and hung over the doorway and windows of your home will provide protection from malocchio and from those with ill-intent entering.

Protection Balm

During the Winter Solstice — the longest night of the year — we often brew up a batch of a protection balm or salve, which can be used to ward those we love from harm; especially useful for those in dangerous lines of work, which these days sadly includes being a medical professional, school teacher or student.

My grandmother would put this balm on her thumb and as she kissed each of us good-bye on the weekends, would anoint our foreheads with a "shmear".

Ingredients:

- 3 Tablespoons of beeswax
- 1/4 cup of camelia seed oil
- 12 drops of patchouli oil
- 9 drops of lavender oil
- 3 drops of lilac oil
- 3 drops of mugwort oil
- 3 drops of hyssop oil

Preparation:

Melt wax into camelia seed oil over a double boiler, when completely blended, remove from heat, and add in the essential oils, blend well, and pour into a four ounce tin.

Placing your hands over the tin (it will be too hot to hold, but you want to do this before it cools) say:

A spell of safety I here cast,
a ward of power to hold us fast.
This shield before, behind,
beside, above and below me

protection binds.

Protezione, potenza e forza!

(Protection, power and strength!)

Keep   tin   sealed   until   ready-to-use.

Daily Protection Oil

For clarity of mind and spiritual protection, we would frequently make up an essential oil that could be worn as a daily protection spell.

Ingredients:

30 ml Extra virgin olive oil or sunflower seed oil

2 drops of cardamom essential oil

2 drops rue essential oil

5 drops rosemary essential oil

5 drops grapefruit essential oil

3 drops bergamot essential oil

7 drops frankincense essential oil

These are blended cold (no heat added) and are placed in an amber or blue coloured bottle, which is then placed on a sunny window sill at sunrise for nine minutes, preferably the first sunrise after the Full Moon.

CHAPTER FIFTEEN

Relationship Spells

There's a common misunderstanding, largely brought about by popular fiction and films, that used to make my Zia Maria get *agita* so often. She would roll her eyes, and bite the back of her hand any time someone came to her and asked her to "do something to make so-and-so fall in love with me," or "help me win [insert cheating, lying husband or boyfriend's name here] back."

She would say, *"L'amore rifiuta di essere legato."* (Love refuses to be bound.)

Love was feral and fluid. And I sense that she probably thought of it in terms that were more Victorian sensibilities, but my Zio Leo would say to me, when I had my first crush on a wonderful gay practitioner of Wicca and Minoan spirituality, with whom I had my first summer fling at sixteen, *"Nessuno cerca di trasformare una tigre selvaggia in un animale domestico."* (No one tries to domesticate a wild tiger.)

So I would come to learn that within our tradition, we would strive not to impose upon the freewill of others, unless it was in defensive posture, or to right an injustice. Therefore, we would not manipulate someone into falling in love with someone else.

We also understood that love often defies logical explanation and breaks its own boundaries with abandon.

Therefore, we didn't impose upon another or manipulate them, because the blow-back and number of things that could go wrong far out-numbered the things that could go well. Instead, we influenced the hearts and minds of others, in a subtle, more nuanced way.

More often than not, what we were doing were healing and transformational spells, designed to bring about harmony, raise awareness of the redeeming qualities of someone, and perhaps, to drive a wedge between those who sought to interfere in, or cause damage to already existing relationships.

This was generally done with dressed candles (which for us, usually meant a glass encased 1-day candle -- similar to the Judaic *yahrtzeit* candle, positioned on a plate, around which *materia magica* was arranged), and some work with allies, correspondences and our Will. We would work with the spiritual allies, saints, plant allies, and ancestors, to bring two people closer together, so that the magic of love itself could potentially do its thing.

Generally speaking, these workings would call into four main categories, examples of which I will share from my original notebooks:

- Bring back a lost or estranged love

- Attracting new love

- Reviving the fire and passion in relationships

- Healing bad blood between people

These spells would generally be done by a solo practitioner, but on occasion, when bringing back someone who was estranged, or in cases of healing bad blood (for example, a relationship in which trust was broken, or infidelity was the issue), it wasn't uncommon for a group of practitioners to work together.

It's also important to understand that from our perspective, love spells were not exclusively about romantic relationships. They could be used to address the same sorts of issues in familial, workplace, platonic, and even supernatural relationships.

Examples of Relationship Spells

Now I am disinclined to offer specific spells for relationships, because the nuance would be missing from them. But instead offer you some components you can use, in conjunction with the Anatomy of a Spell, offered in the beginning of this book, as you see fit.

Folklore suggests that herbs, such as black cohosh, cardamom, cinnamon and clove, as well as plant ancestors such as jasmine, lavender, orange blossom and rose can help us to create the energetic conditions to heal relationships.

Making candles or balms with these ingredients has always been part of the Afro-Sicilian magical tradition. Placing these ingredients into a small santuccio pouch, and wearing it around your neck is another way of drawing on this energy.

Among the older traditions, probably drawing on the ancient lore of our African ancestors, we place offerings to the Oldest of the Ancestors, including watermellon and sugarcane syrup, to draw the nurturing and protective energy of the Archetypal Mothers (like Yemayá).

I am personally convinced of this ancient African connection, as the ritual we would most often perform, would involve placing one blue and one white pillar candle (glass votives) on either side of the Blessed Mother Stella Maris, and arrange seven white flowers, seven silver dollars, and a small bowl of sugar cane syrup, which sat over a folded paper with our relationship intention written in beet juice.

During one of my relationships in my mid-twenties, the two men with whom I was in relationship invited me to their godmother's home, who was a respected santera. She performed a ritual to bless our relationship and home, which was almost identical to the one I did, described above. The guys laughed, when they saw the look on my face, because they insisted the

Afro-Sicilian tradition was just another form of *Regla Lucumí*. That would become a rabbit hole I found irresistible, and which I would later discover was not far from the truth.

Old Ways Finding New Audiences

Not long ago, I ran across a spell in an Associated Press article from Ho Chi Min, Vietnam! It was almost identical to a spell we've used to strengthen relationships, which we would perform as our nightly fire began to die down.

You need laurel leaves and a dying fire to perform this ritual. Find a comfortable spot and sit before the dying fire. Gaze into the burning fire, calm your mind, and focus on the thoughts related to your love interest only. Place a small basket of laurel leaves between your knees. While staring at the fire, take a handful of leaves out of the basket; then, throw them onto the dying fire and wait for them to burst into flames.

As they do, say out loud:

" *Laurel leaves are burning in the fire. Please send my wish to the universe and draw renewed love to my life.* "

Finally, wait until the flame dies down and repeat all the steps above again 3 times.

CHAPTER SIXTEEN

Spiritual Afflictions - An Old World Perspective

The final few chapters of this book are excerpts from fifteen years of journals, beginning when I was sixteen, and continuing through my thirtieth birthday. It was during this period of time that I was more deeply immersed in the "mysteries" that the men in the Afro-Sicilian and Southern Italian traditions would study and discuss.

Often these concepts were unpacked around a nightly fire in the backyard, while spending summers at the Jersey Shore. As different uncles, cousins and other relatives would visit, the women would often play Pokeno — a popular American game, which combined elements of poker and keno, the rules of which Italian-Americans often "modified" so as to seek out some divination results, through the cards dealt and played.

The men would eventually join the women at times, and other times, would talk well into the night around the fire, which was often made in a large oil-drum, propped up on cinder blocks, in which various plant materia might be added, to assist in the *penetrazione* (or insight) that might derive from from what amounts to a bit of fire scrying.

I say that these journal entries mostly came from the summers, because those were the times when I would initially be on summer break from seminary, or on holiday from my parish assignments; but there are also a fair number of key contributions which came from the contemplative monks, priests and nuns, who served as my "old world mentors", whom we referred to as *i custodi dei segreti* — the Keepers of the Secrets. These were a community of Sicilian, North African, Greek, Basque and Romani practitioners, who lived a consecrated life, "hiding in plain sight" as it were, to protect our ways from falling into the wrong hands.

There is unquestionably a great deal of what I learned from these practitioners, which like what I learned in my family practice, doesn't feel appropriate to simply expose in a book. That's one of the principal reasons I created the Inner Alchemy Mystery School — a place where I could teach the next generation of teachers, in a way that allowed me to personally connect with those I felt were ready to take their spiritual and esoteric practice to a different place.

And that's where this book was so hard to finalise. First, because I could have included another 100,000 words, just covering the spellwork and plant magic that were part of my tradition over these past fifty years. Second, because the "mysteries" could fill another 150,000 words, just based on my journals and personal experience.

That seemed like it would have been too much for anyone to really digest, especially without personal, one-on-one mentorship, like I make available to students in the Mystery School.

So, an abridged version, which would have value and use for all who picked up this book was my objective; knowing that those who were ready to dig deeper could reach out to me, or to my successors in the Mystery School. And that brings me to a matter that I will briefly touch on in this section, because I want this book to remain about the ancestors and their contributions to the ways that have been woven into my personal spiritual practice, and the practices of a couple hundred folks I have had the privilege to personally mentor... not about me.

At the time of the publication of this book, some thirty-nine years after I was first diagnosed with AIDS (back when it was not yet even called AIDS, but rather GRID - Gay-Related Immune Deficiency), which already seemed like a lot to deal with, on top of living with seizure disorder (that came and went, and was mostly very mild, until recent years) and seminary formation... Fifteen years after my diagnosis with AIDS-related Parkinsonism... I am dealing with new, and by some accounts, more serious medical issues.

The prognosis is not something I am willing to commit to writing, nor are the specifics of the condition something I will be detailing here for the reasons stated, as well as for the reasons of warding and protecting myself, as I undertake what will undoubtedly be an intense period of spiritual work and healing journey — no matter the physical outcome.

I don't seek pity or want any reader to waste a moment on sadness over this revelation, because I assure you that I have the matter well at-hand. And if the old stories of my grandmother, great aunts and great uncles are to believed, these "spiritual afflictions" were always foretold to be part of my personal journey. So, I don't invest any energy into the "why me" concerns that might come with difficult medical diagnoses and their accompanying issues. Instead, I prefer to allow this news to become a "teachable moment" — something of a backdrop against which I can share these journal entries, in a way that tells a bit of a story of how our people viewed illness and dis-ease as "spiritual afflictions", and how that figured into the ways we go about working our ways to heal and produce better outcomes in the face of such illnesses.

Understanding My Vocabulary

When approaching this section, I realised that there were a considerable number of terms that we use in the Afro-Sicilian tradition, which might be confusing to those who are from outside the culture, or who grew up in a more Americanised culture, even if they were Italian or Sicilian.

So, I've attempted to use English words that are somewhat more utilitarian, and hopefully somewhat more universally understood for two reasons. The first is that it will make it clearer, when looking at how the worldview that we spoke about in the early chapters of this book fits in with our approach to living a healthy, vital and meaningful life.

And second, I've chosen terms that allow room for personal nuance and gnosis. That means that you and I might understand generally what a term means, but you might have some considerable insights that differ from mine, in your own personal spiritual tradition. Your own ancestors will have influenced and helped guide you in developing your relationship to the cosmos, and I do not wish to interfere in that process of unfolding.

So, you will be able to apply your deeper meanings to the things I share, and that will, I think, make this material even richer for you!

Here are a few of the terms I will use throughout this section and what I mean generally by them:

Source - Our worldview is one which embraces what we call Essential Unity, meaning that at our deepest, most highly distilled and fundamental nature, we are all made up of the same energy as everything else in the cosmos. Science has born this out. You and I are made of the same stuff that the stars are made of, and therefore, are as ancient and primordial. Our physical bodies are transient, temporary and impermanent vehicles, but the "stuff" we are made of is essentially ONE. And so I refer to this Oneness as Source. It's the Creative Intelligence and the Love from which all things manifest; which the ancient Buddhists refer to as "Emptiness" or Śunyata; the Sikh's call it **"Ek Ong Kar"**; other primitive cultures would anthropomorphise this concept into their respective religious deities; and Einstein would refer to it as "the zero-point". It is both the source of our being, and the source of our power as practitioners.

Chaotic Data - The unconscious data or conditioning that plays itself out both in our own body-minds and those of others, which seldom has any relationship to the way things actually happened or exist. For example, in the years that follow a terrible argument, which may have resulted in our parting ways with someone we care about, we often tend to colour in the details of that argument, over time, with data that is entirely born out of our fears and anger. So the memory is no longer an accurate memory. It's been corrupted by our biases, fears, anger and other conditioning. That is chaotic data.

Unconditional Responsibility - When we truly live within our power, we understand that everything we experience in this holographic universe is a direct out-picturing of the beliefs we hold, the fears we entertain, and the chaotic data we've allowed to permeate our minds. Unconditional Responsibility is a mindset which consciously chooses to accept the responsibility for our experiences, and see them as opportunities for us to grow and heal.

As a metaphysical concept, Unconditional Responsibility is paradoxical on two levels. The first paradox is that its methods cannot be communicated except by using the very chaotic data that we seek to eliminate from our worldview.

This is because by nature, philosophical and metaphysical concepts draw on data; they use language, which is stored in memory. And we know the memories may have been interpreted through a corrupt lens.

So, we use techniques, spellwork and other elements of our Craft to manipulate and shift the energy around a situation, cause or condition, to influence and affect the outcome.

These are useful approaches up until the point that we finally "get it", at which point the need for formal and rote spellwork becomes less necessary, and we simply live in our power.

There is a story in Buddhist traditions and in the stories of the Catholic mystics, which tells of a metaphysical "raft", which takes us from the shores of delusion and suffering to a place of calm abiding or "zero-point", where such constructs themselves no longer become necessary.

Perhaps these journal entries can serve as such a raft for the reader.

Source Always Accepts What We Choose to Believe

In the Kybalion the first principle is stated as, "The All is Mind; the Universe is Mental." I remember having a bit of a laugh reading that, while studying advanced hair design with Trevor Sorbie, in Lamb's Conduit, on London's East End, because "mental" had a completely different meaning there! But this fundamental truth was something I was taught early on.

I learned that what I believe, including what I feared (because fear is a reflection of the beliefs we have that are rooted in chaotic data), always became true for me.

Source didn't judge me or criticise me for my beliefs. It simply made them manifest. And science would later begin to understand that a bit of real magic occurs in the brain's pre-frontal cortex, where our statements, beliefs and thoughts are "heard" and begin to be manifest at the most subtle level.

Immediately, this clicked for me, as I wrote in my journal:

This almost seems too simple. Universal Mind responds to every thought, every belief, every fear and every statement we make, and begins to manifest those things into our experience. It's almost as though we live on a holodeck, like Star Trek, and Source is the Programmer!

I'm beginning to understand that what we call magic, and Zio Leo refers to as "The Craft of the Wise" is literally this Wisdom. We think a thought, or hold fast to a belief, and the Universe conspires with us to make it so. Why isn't this something every world religion teaches?!?

Our Parents' View of the World Isn't Always Right

Zia Irenelle would say that my parents were doing the best they knew how, but that it wasn't ever going to be enough for me. "They interpret the world through their fears, their beliefs, and their own childhood experiences," she would tell me, while we drove from Mystic Island (on the Jersey Shore) back to Philadelphia for the week, "And that's why they struggle so much… they're creating a world that reflects all the pain and fear that their childhoods brought them."

Of course, my Aunt Irene didn't really understand concepts like trauma, in the way we now do, but she nailed it. I would reflect in my journal:

Zia Irenelle said she would help me to live a better life than my parents created for themselves. She said it's not their fault, because no one would choose a life of struggle, but they both had tough childhoods and teen-age years. "If they knew better, they would have created better lives."

I am realising that this world is not what I was taught. So much of what I learned to think and believe about the world, even from Zia Irenelle, is interpreted through the lens of their experiences. I think I must do that too. But I was given this extraordinary chance to change my perspective, and I think that's why I am different from every one of my siblings and cousins.

It's like the only thing we're dealing with is energy, and energy expresses itself in my mind as thought. So, what I am forever dealing with in life isn't everyone else, it's my own thoughts, beliefs and fears! And thoughts, beliefs and fears can be changed. Here we are again... the Source of Magic is **thought**!

Some thoughts are based on stuff that we think happened, but which might not have really happened. For example, whenever it's time to leave the Island for the week, my heart is so sad because I won't get to hang around with Jeffrey and Danny, and most of all with my cousin, Bobby. And in my head, I just want to tell them how much I love them, but I know they will think I am just being queer. So, I think I am very awkward around them on Sunday afternoons.

But really, they probably don't even notice, and so I create this whole scene in my head that didn't really happen, and I base my future decisions on what I "believe" happened, but it's all chaotic data as Uncle Tootsie would say.

Chaotic data! Yes! That's what our ways are designed to fix.

Maybe malocchio isn't something someone else does to us, but something we do to ourselves, because we believe that they gave us the "look". And so, we remove it, by shifting the energy and that allows us the space to believe it's being taken away, which manifests in our experience!

Maybe the same thing happens at Mass. We believe there is a miracle taking place at the altar that allows us to commune with Source, but what really happens is that we shift the energy that allows us to remember that we are ALWAYS connected with Source. THAT is Communion.

Unconditional Responsibility and Magic

It was the end of my seventeenth summer, and I started to get it:

This was an amazing summer. I think I get it now. It's all about unconditional responsibility. That's all magic and witchcraft really is. I mean sure, Zio Leo has some mythological religious rituals that are part of his practice that we don't always understand, but we have our own religious rituals, and all of it really seems to be about the same thing... learning to take unconditional responsibility for what unfolds in our experiences.

I think it's less about doing a spell for someone else, and more about doing a spell to get right with my own mind, so that it's in perfect alignment with Source. Then the magic is what happens. It has to happen, because it's always happening!

And there is a synergy between us and the plant ancestors, and the ancient ancestors of the earth itself. That's why the Elixir works. It's why the medicine works. All of it is about essential unity and unconditional responsibility.

So that's what Mimi means, when she says that illness is a "spiritual affliction" we can learn to work out! It really is!

Three years later, that realisation would shift a bit into higher gear, as I was no longer spending my summers in South Jersey, but was living as a Franciscan contemplative in Fort Lauderdale. My teenage crush on the beautiful and influential "puppy love" I had for Eddie Buczynski had given way to a friendship that no longer included sexual trysts, and that allowed him and me to have much richer conversations about these things — conversations that would end up saving my life, after the fateful events of May 10th, in 1983.

Things Falling Apart and Coming Together

In the early morning hours of May 10th, 1983, shortly after midnight, I was walking home from a part-time job I had to help cover the expenses of our newly formed friary in Fort Lauderdale, Florida. I was working as a security guard for a condo in Hollywood, Florida — a perfect job it seemed, since I was left alone all night, from 10 PM until 7 AM, allowing me to study and read most of the night, since the majority of residents there were older.

But the security supervisor, without my knowing, was listening into my phone conversations with other members of the friary, and he quickly realised that I was gay and genderqueer. So he fired me, and ranted about how this company didn't need another degenerate working for him.

Now South Florida didn't have the best public transportation late at night, so I figured that I was fit enough to make the roughly eleven mile walk home, given that I walked about nine miles a day for exercise anyway. And so, I headed up U.S. Highway 1, toward SE 7th Street, wearing my security guard uniform, and carrying a bag with some books and my habit in it. I usually changed back into my Franciscan habit at the end of my shift, but this time I was summarily thrown out the door, and would have to just endure the scratchy polyester uniform pants and stiff shirt for a few more hours.

As I walked, I was aware of the rage I was feeling over being marginalised and called a "degenerate" by the supervisor. I felt discarded and once again felt like I was never going to find a place that would truly welcome me as a queer person.

My thoughts were interrupted by a group of four men who stepped out from between a couple buildings, just ahead of me.

They were probably a little drunk, from their slurred speech, and were speaking what I originally thought was French, until I began hearing it more clearly, and realised was Creole. These men were Haitians, and probably among the so-called "boat people" who were sent away from their country, and treated to a horrible, xenophobic and biased lack of hospitality in South Florida during those years.

To make a nightmarish experience brief, the men apparently thought I was a cop, and had likely been abused by cops in the area, as I had personally witnessed such disgraceful injustices being visited upon the Haitians myself. And these men were apparently pushed to their limits, because although I only understood about half of what was being said to me, since I spoke French, but not Creole, they were going to "show me what it was like".

Over the next hour, I was savagely raped, beaten, and abused at gunpoint in the lot behind a 7-Eleven store. A gun, pointed at my right temple, was fired when they were done, and apparently misfired, leaving only powder burns and doing slight nerve damage to the skin that remains to this day.

I was in shock, and when the rape centre finished processing me, I was sent to the Hollywood Police Station, where I was unable to identify any of the assailants, and where the cop who was taking my statement said it sounded like, "one of those faggot fantasies that just got a little out of control". He was convinced I asked for it, and that somehow, all of this was just another example of why they shouldn't allow "my kind of people" in South Florida.

And in the months that followed, I began to realise that I was manifesting in my experience a deeply held belief about being marginalised, disparaged, and a "stranger in a strange land".

That didn't mean I was to blame for what happened, but it meant I had the key to be able to put all of this behind me... until I woke up with 104 fever one morning in November that year, and wound up at Jackson Memorial Hospital, in the isolation ward, where I was diagnosed as having a rare type of pneumonia, and diagnosed as having GRID - Gay Related Immune Deficiency (the term used before it would later come to be known as AIDS).

Things were falling apart, as I was told I would likely die within the next 18-24 months... but that was also when all that seemed to be falling apart started coming together for me personally and magically.

Another Perspective from Outside Our Ways

It was shortly thereafter that I met Dr. Louise L. Hay and Dr. Kennedy Shultz, and began to learn the perspective of the New Thought Community, which seemed to almost seamlessly blend with our tradition, especially when it came to their approach to dis-ease (a lack of ease in the body, which has its roots in the mind).

Now my meeting and working with Louise Hay was mostly in the context of her weekly sessions with other gay people who were diagnosed with AIDS, in West Hollywood (California), which were known as "Hay Rides". But prior to the epidemic, her focus was broader, and included self-esteem, finances, relationships, and other issues that cause people to become disconnected from their personal power.

And I definitely had issues with her approach at times, which eventually led me to part ways with her; while still being grateful for having had the chance to see connections in other traditions, such as the Science of Mind, with the ancient wisdom of my ancestral tradition. Moving to Atlanta, I connected with a friend of hers, Dr. Kennedy Shultz, and found in Ken a friend with whom I could spend hours over coffee, connecting the dots between my ancestral/hereditary tradition, and the more strictly secular approach taken by New Thought. (Again, I had issue with some

New Thought traditions, which tended toward using religious terminology, such as "God", in their approach, but Ken guided me toward what was then a separate and more rational/secular movement that arose out of the "churchy" Science of Mind groups, and it was a period of growth and healing.

What it did for me was to allow me to see that there is a universality of our approach that I previously thought might not have existed.

I mean, when you think about it, I was surrounded by people who were involved in the pop-culture, neo-pagan version of the Craft, where conflation of the Old Religion with the actual magical traditions of the ancient cultures were so problematic that I was beginning to think there were no practitioners outside of my family and a few other Italian families who understood the difference.

I had nothing against neo-paganism. Nothing at all. But I wasn't interested in a 20th century religion, and often found its practitioners were not secure enough in their practice to accept it for what it is — a 20th century reconstructionist approach, combining the imagined practices of the Old Religious Cults of Diana, Hekate, and others, with 19th and 20th century occultism, Freemasonry, and Crowley's musings, and an imaginative approach to magic that drew mostly on the colourful and rich British Isles' folk magic traditions. The need to pretend that their traditions today have roots in the ancient groves of Tuscany, or in Sicily is not just annoying — it's grotesque cultural appropriation that is unsupported by even the slightest anthropological or historic evidence.

My working with Ken Shultz and the community of his Atlanta Religious Science Centre helped me to see that our traditions did actually survive and make their way into the melting pot of mainstream culture and spirituality — just not into the world of pop-culture neo-paganism.

(There was one notable exception, and that can be found in many of those whose works I've recommended in this book, who studied with Salem's Laurie Cabot, whose approach was much less reliant upon the neo-pagan mythology, and more rooted in the mastery of the mind and personal power. That powerful approach, which can then be blended with the religious motifs of various traditions, exists in some of those neo-pagan practitioners whose work I most admire, including Chris Penczak, Mat Auryn, Storm Faerywolf, Chris Allaun, and Devin Hunter, to name a few.)

In the section that follows, I am including a section of my journals that were the result of painstakingly merging older entries (from 1979-1981) with notes taken during conversations with Louise Hay and Kennedy Shultz (1983-1993).

These are a series of health conditions that were considered to be physical evidence of "spiritual afflictions" in the Afro-Sicilian magical tradition. I have only included those conditions for which I have personally witnessed effective transformation, healing and release, using our approach. It's worth pointing out again that my intention is not to diagnose, treat, nor make curative medical claims in this book. The information shared from my journals is offered for educational consideration only.

How to Use this Section

Within the following pages, I will share a considerable number of conditions that manifest in our lives, followed by a brief explanation of how my ancestors and family would approach the spiritual affliction we believed to be "behind" the illness or condition.

The purpose of this grimoire, start to finish, as indicated by the title, is to bring about personal healing and transformation. I believe this material can unlock some of those processes for you, but the depth of the healing and transformation will be entirely brought about by the amount of work you're willing to put into it.

So just let this serve as a "diving-off point", and let your intuition, and the wisdom of *your ancestors* take you on the healing journey that follows.

Not every entry has a "spell" per se, but by using the Anatomy of a Spell, as described earlier, we would approach healing by addressing the issues that led the body to the imbalances that created the causes of these afflictions.

It's also important to understand that this section is not saying, for example, that AIDS is directly caused by anger, or that Alzheimer's is caused by anger left unresolved. The idea of the ancestors was that common illnesses were outward appearances that the body had become run down by spiritual afflictions, which allowed the disease process to progress.

So if, for example, we're in a constant state of anger, and do not express it, we never give the mind a chance to relax. This will certainly cause hormonal and chemical imbalances in the body, especially in the brain, which can set the stage for depletion of important hormones, such as DHEA, and that in turn could create conditions favourable for cognitive decline.

Abscesses

An abscess is evidence of something energetically fermenting within the body. We see this condition arise when we become eaten-up with anger or the need for revenge.

Spell: Grind dried wormwood into a powder and sprinkle it over the top of a white pillar candle, which has been placed on a fire-safe plate (or a sea salt filled bowl) around which six holly leaves are arranged. Using the formula outlined in the *Anatomy of a Spell* section of this book, shift the energy around the condition by stating that you release any and all patterns that bind you with anger. Allow the plant ancestors of wormwood to send back the poison that allowed the abscess to manifest to the person(s) who caused the problems.

Aches

When we feel aching in our body, especially muscle aches, it's an indication that we are experiencing unresolved need to be held, comforted or loved. It's important to remember, taking Unconditional Responsibility, we are the ones responsible for loving and nurturing ourselves… no one else. When we do so, others will respond with love and affection to us, because we will have affirmed in Consciousness that we are worthy of loving.

Spell: Prepare a tea of spearmint and chamomile, sweetened with honey. Sit at the table where you do your ancestral work, and allow yourself to feel the love of all of those who came before you. Recognise that you are worthy of love, and that it begins with choosing to love yourself.

Acne

Some acne, such as pubescent acne, has its roots in hormonal imbalances. But we can further extrapolate that those hormonal imbalances are often the cause of teenage angst and low self-esteem; therefore, when we experience acne as adults, it's a sign of the same imbalances, which we believe are actually caused by lacking self-acceptance and poor self-esteem.

Spell: Select a musical piece (preferably without lyrics) or Solfeggio frequencies that resonate with deep feelings of love and peace. Remind yourself that you are worthy of love and acceptance, exactly as you are. Connect with the Sacred Within, and then prepare an edible spell by grinding some calendula, lavender and chamomile into a powder, and add it to a couple tablespoons of olive oil. Squeeze in the juice of one lemon and eat over a salad of field greens. When you are done, take a piece of cotton cloth or cotton ball, and sop-up some of the remaining oil, lemon and herbal dressing. Dab it on the acne breakout, and allow it to sit for 15 minutes. Rinse and blot, being mindful not to touch the area for at least an hour.

Addiction

This one is a biggie, and one that science and psychology has come to affirm what our ancestors have believed for generations. Addiction arises from fear — not of our weaknesses, but of our innate power. That fear manifests as painful thoughts, memories, or bodily aches (see the section on aches, above), and so we react to those conditions by attempting to run from or medicate ourselves out of dealing with them. In essence, we have forgotten how to love ourselves and forgive ourselves, and addiction becomes the escape from that responsibility.

Spell: This spell takes nine nights to perform, and a full lunar cycle to complete its work.

Obtain two candles, one black and one white. If you are working on behalf of someone else, then acquire a lock of hair, fingernails or, if that isn't possible, a picture or an object they've touched.

Place that personal item by the white candle at the centre of your altar, or on a window sill. Set the black candle next to it, toward the nearest window.

On a small sheet of paper, write down the outcome you desire as if it's already a fact. So, if you intend to stop using cocaine, write, "I am free of any desires for drugs. Cocaine has no appeal or power over me." Or, if you are trying to quit smoking, write, "I am free from my addiction to cigarettes." If casting the spell for someone else, then just use their full name in the third person: "Susanna Colletti is clean and sober."

Tear up the page into nine pieces, crumpling them up, and then arranging them in a row next to the black candle, heading west or toward the nearest window.

Light both candles. Meditate, visualising the feeling of freedom from your vices, and then burn the paper nearest the black candle. Move the black candle one space away from the white candle, so it sits behind the second piece of crumpled paper. Extinguish the black candle and then the white one.

On the next night, meditate upon your outcome again, and when you're done, burn the next piece of paper. Move the black candle one more space away from the white candle. In this manner, continue for nine nights, each night meditating upon the outcome you desire, burning one of the pieces of paper, and moving the black candle another space away from the white candle. Continue until all of the pieces of paper have been burned, and the black candle and white candle are far apart from one another. You may need multiples of each candle to burn for enough nights, unless you use pillar candles, which I recommend.

Take the remnants of the spell—the ash from the burnt paper, and any candle wax that may be remaining—and bury them somewhere out in nature, far from your home.

AIDS/HIV

Of course, when I was younger, this entry in my journals originally came under the heading of leukemia and immune disorders. After my being raped, when I was diagnosed with AIDS, Louise Hay suggested that I begin working with the condition by considering the acronym as meaning, "Anger Incorrectly Directed at the Self".

Immune deficiencies often arise from not feeling like we are safe or protected, and our justified anger at those who have failed us becomes turned inward. (In my case, I did the whole, "If I wouldn't have been walking down that road on May 10th, I would never have been raped, and wouldn't have gotten AIDS" routine.)

Releasing self-blame, and all that kills our inspiration in life is the key to releasing the impact that this condition has on our lives.

(Note that we're not talking about curing a disease. We're talking about healing the impact the condition has on our lives. It's currently been 39 years since I first developed the pneumocystis carinii pneumonia and cytomegalovirus that resulted in my full-blown AIDS diagnosis. And despite all the cocktails, drug therapies, etc., I still have full-blown AIDS, and my immune system has, periodically, been almost non-existent. But I've used this approach to minimise the impact living with AIDS has on my life, and as a result, remain the longest surviving person in North America with full-blown AIDS, almost four decades in.)

Spell: On a firesafe plate, place a candle with one or two drops of Strega Oil placed near the wick. Arrange tulsi leaves or rue around the base of the candle. State, using the formula of the *Anatomy of a Spell*, that you are safe, and release any anger directed at yourself or others. Reclaim your personal power, and declare your willingness and innate ability to protect yourself and stand strong against whatever challenges come your way. Allow the candle to burn for six hours or more and extinguish or allow to burn out naturally.

Alzheimer's Disease/Dementia

When we allow fear and suppressed anger to build, we begin to respond to life with resistance. Dementia and forgetfulness, and mental conditions such as Alzheimer's are evidence that we refuse to accept the world as it is. It can also be a refusal to work through terrible traumas that we experienced or believe we might have experienced.

Spell: For this spell, we have to call on the plant ancestors to fortify us to forgive and let go of the past. This can be achieved by setting aside 30-minutes each day for a full lunar cycle, beginning on the Balsamic (Waning Crescent) moon, during which we sit with a cup of lemon balm and spearmint tea, pouring one cup for ourselves and one for the ancestors.

Sit comfortably, and choose to think of all of those who have loved and supported you in your life, allowing a feeling of forgiveness and healing to wash over you.

Anemia

Afflicted by not feel up-to-the-task of claiming our place in the world, the body will often begin to exhibit signs of anemia.

Spell: Hang an iron horseshoe, open end facing down, to keep evil spirits out of your home, and take back your power. A horseshoe found along the side of a road is particularly powerful, and was known to provide protection against disease.

Anxiety

This affliction arises from not trusting the flow and process of life. When we forget our power and connection to its Source, we become anxious.

Spell: You will need:

- A black candle – you need to let this candle burn down to

nothing in this spell. Choose a candle that has an appropriate burn time. If you are in a hurry, choose a smaller candle with less burn time.

- Banishing oil – (Banishing Oil is made on the night of the Balsamic Moon, by taking three pinches of Banishing Dust, and adding it to a 30-40ml bottle, into which equal parts of sunflower and castor oil are added. An eighth tsp of vodka or grain alcohol is added, and the whole thing mixed up and allowed to "cure" for 30 days.)

- A fire-proof bowl

- A small ritual knife or pin. I've been using a pin to carve my candles with recently. I was using a ritual knife but changed because I find the pin easier to work with.

Steps:

1. Find a space where you will be undisturbed. Gather all your ingredients in front of you.

2. Take your black candle and use your pin to carve any words or symbols (sigils) relating to your anxiety onto the candle. For example, anxiety, fear, stress, anger, nervousness, angst, apprehension, doubt, concern, dread, uncertainty and distress.

3. Anoint your candle with your banishing oil. A few drops are enough.

4. Holding your candle, close your eyes and take 5 deep, long breaths. Try and find a small calm spot in the sea of your anxiety and anchor yourself there.

5. With your eyes still closed, direct all of your feelings of anxiety into the candle. Imagine it like a sponge, soaking up all the negative energy in your body. Think about the words you carved into you candle and focus on how it would feel if those feelings disappeared. Let your candle

absorb the negative feelings that cause your anxiety and imagine them being gently released from your body and mind and moving into the candle. Open your eyes.

6.   Take your candle and place it in the fire-proof bowl. If you are using a taper, melt the bottom of the candle a little so that it sticks to the bottom of the bowl.

7.   Light your candle.

8.   Look into the flame and imagine it transforming all the anxiety you just channeled into the candle into positive energy. Watch the flame as it consumes the wax and imagine that the flame is the power within you. This power provides you with light, warmth and comfort while warding off negativity, consuming the anxiety and releasing it from your experience.

9.   Make sure your candle is in a safe place and allow it to burn down until it goes out on its own. If you don't have time to let it burn out, let it burn as long as you can and then use a candle snuffer to put out the flame. Don't use this candle again in another spell.

10.   Take any remnants of wax from the candle and bury or dispose of them away from your home.

Repeat this ritual as often as you need it.

Arthritis

Feeling unloved or unappreciated. Resentment over the way we're being treated can lead to swelling joints, feeling old or no longer useful.

Tea: A treatment taken for 60-days, made from ginger, turmeric and willow bark helps release the resentment, and has been shown to scientifically reduce inflammation.

Asthma

When we are made to feel smothered by someone who is overly controlling, or feel like our right to express ourselves is being stifled, we set the stage for asthma and breathing problems.

Spell: Take a small bowl, like a finger-bowl, and fill it with sea salt. Place in it a coin that you've carried in your pocket for a couple hours.

As you place the coin into the salt, say:

"I have fashioned you, and your name is _____. You shall receive the negative energy sent by _____ in my place."

Set the bowl out of the way some place for 30-days.

At the end of the thirty days, dump the contents of the bowl, including the coin, into a hole somewhere near the edge of your property, and light a white candle over the hole after filling it back in. As the candle burns down, the control the person has will burn off in the fire, and you will be able to breathe easier.

Back Pain

Our backs represent the structures that give support to our lives. Lower back indicates feeling unsupported financially. Mid-back represents carrying guilt. Upper back is where we carry the burdens of others we've taken on.

Spellwork: Nothing works better for this sort of affliction than a cleansing spiritual bath, with Epsom salts and eucalyptus. Add a couple bay leaves for lower back issues, some rue for mid-back issues, and rose for upper back issues.

Balance Issues

When our thoughts are off-centre and scattered, and when our efforts are not focused, we may experience balance issues. We treat this with mindfulness and by taking care to re-centre ourselves.

Bleeding

Bleeding is an affliction that arises out of uncontrolled anger and a loss of desire to live. We can see how someone who is listless, maybe angst and overcome with anger, might accidentally cut themselves cooking. This is one of the reasons we never cook anything while angry or fearful, because we see those energies as poisons that can be transferred to the food.

Spell: There is no greater spell for alleviating a lack of joy in life than to walk barefoot on the grass, or along the sandy shores of the ocean. But we can also allow ourselves to watch the joy and playfulness of children, or puppies, kittens, etc. to energetically remind us of our connection to our joy.

Blood Pressure

It's critically important to restate that the intention of this guide is not to become a substitution for medical care. However, in the ancient ways of our ancestors, we viewed high blood pressure as evidence of long-standing problems that were left unresolved, while low blood pressure pointed to unresolved childhood issues of not feeling loved, appreciated or valued.

Spell: ***Ritual bath for releasing unresolved emotional blockages***

1 cup of Epsom salts

1/2 cup of sea salt

Grind up some dried lavender, geranium, rosemary and rue with mortar and pestal and add 1/2 teaspoon of heated olive oil to the mixture. Allow to sit for 30 minutes.

Then draw a warm bath, and add the oil (with the dried flower bits still intact), and the salts.

Soak for 30 minutes or longer, while taking slow, deep breaths.

Bronchitis

Depending on which side of the family you asked, bronchitis was either a manifestation of feeling like one couldn't take in life fully (feeling oppressed) or the result of not being able to express who we really are, due to concerns about how the family would react.

I find both explanations worth consideration, and highly intersectional. And they are related to the next condition as well, both of which can be resolved with the same working.

Cataracts

When we don't want to see things as they really are, that denial is said to create the conditions for cataracts in our lives.

Spellwork: The best resolutions for the issues of feeling like we cannot take in life or express it fully, and not wanting to see things as they truly are come from cord-cutting from those things that bind us. Whether it's a cleansing bath, malocchio removal, knotwork, or banishing rituals, we can benefit from severing those toxic ties.

Chills

When we experience the chills, it's said that someone from among the ancestors is trying to get through to us. If we've cultivated a meaningful ancestral practice, we can resolve this by sitting quietly and inviting them in. If not, we can turn to someone with divination skills and ask them for insight.

Fever

Anger, uncontrolled and/or bottled up will always express as fever, or "fever blisters" (such as cold sores).

Spell: The spellwork done to release bottled up anger can be used to heal any conditions in this section, with modification as needed.

Ingredients:

- One blue candle

- Six cloves

Preparation:

1. Dress the candle with six cloves (if working with a pillar candle, place them in a circle around the candle, or pierce the candle, pushing them into the candle; when working with a glass votive candle, arrange them in a circle around the base of the candle, which should be placed on a fire-safe plate).

2. Charge the candle by drawing out the love and healing energy from your heart-centre and energising it, saying, "I consecrate and charge this candle as a physical tool for healing and representation of the healing that is already underway on the ethereal plane."

3. Next focus on healing rising up within you, touching every place in your life that there is anger or fear. Envision that healing spreading out from the top of your head to the area surrounding you, and then in ripples, generating wave-after-wave of healing that reaches everyone you know and don't know.

4. If there is a specific person for whom you are doing this working, picture them being enveloped in this wave of healing energy as well.

5.   Say, "Magic mend and candle burn, anger end, and peace return."

6.   Let the candle burn until it goes out on its own.

Other Conditions

Apply the ritual above to the following conditions, adding the specific essential oil mentioned after the "spiritual affliction" to the candle (one or two drops) before lighting, and adapt the magical declaration to fit that situation or condition.

Infection - Unresolved Anger ("Magic mend and candle burn, anger end, and peace return.") Add 2 drops of oregano oil to the candle.

Inflammation - Inflamed fires of anger or resentment ("Magic mend and candle burn, anger end, and peace return.") Add 2 drops of bergamot or rose oil to the candle.

Kidney Issues - Unwillingness to let go of toxic relationships ("Magic mend and candle burn, I now let go, and peace returns.") Add 2 drops of bergamot or rose oil to the candle.

Knee Issues - Inflexibility, not trusting in your ability to move in the right direction ("Magic mend and fire's reflection, move me in the right direction.") Add 2 drops of ylang ylang or bergamot oil to the candle.

Nervousness - Fear, which is the opposite of love. We can only operate from one or the other energy. ("Magic mend and candle burns, fear dissolves, and peace returns.") Add 2 drops of rose oil to the candle.

Stomach Problems - Inability to digest what's going on ("Magic mend and candle burn, *agita* leaves, clarity returns.") Add 2 drops of chamomile oil to the candle.

With this final section of this grimoire, I hope to have planted the seeds that will allow the germination of the wisdom and indwelling "knowing" that will allow you to one day set aside the need for anything more than your own perfect and powerful magic to guide you.

As with anything, there are spells that require more instruction than can be conveyed in writing. We provide that subtle nuance and personal mentoring in our courses at the Inner Alchemy Mystery School.

Additionally, there are powerful spells for personal empowerment, bodily autonomy, gender affirmation, racial injustices, and crushing those who bring us harm that could simply not be properly detailed in this volume. Whenever such a need exists, I try to make myself available to be of assistance in any way possible.

Conclusion

Writers and teachers begin with specific ends in mind. The approximate number of words, chapters and sections of a book are among these. Topics to be covered are also considered.

That's normally an easy part of the writing process for me. But this volume was a greater challenge than I think I've ever encountered.

In part, I think that was because I knew that I needed to fit in almost four decades of spellcraft and practice into approximately 50,000 words, in order to keep the costs in line with the intended price-point. Few authors talk about that, but in today's economy, it was a realistic part of calculating how deeply I could dive in a single book.

Another consideration for this particular book was the feeling of urgency that came from an unexpected bit of medical news that increased my need to convey "the important stuff" now, before potential health and cognitive issues become a mitigating factor.

And then there is the simple issue of loving what I've been privileged to do for these past forty-plus years so much, that I could simply fill volumes with the sorts of workings that make up our worldview and travels through our daily lives.

I do hope that I will have other opportunities to write, to teach and to speak with those who travel these roads of the Unnamed Path. But whether or not that occurs, it's my most sincere wish that this little book will have had value for each and every reader, meeting them at the point of their personal and metaphysical need.

Thank you for allowing me that opportunity.

Blessings on your journey!

Gianmichael Salvato

Afterword

Authenticity is a word that I hear being thrown around a lot by people of my generation (I'm a Millennial). We want the most authentic connections, we want the most authentic practice, but we forget that the first step to authenticity is to be authentic and true to ourselves and our own path ahead.

Gianmichael has presented in the pages that you've just read a way to authenticity, a way to connect with your own power and your own spiritual path, in a time where so much of the magical works and marketing that wants to teach us how to be carbon copies of other peoples' paths, other names and cults of personalities, that teach us if we only follow the formula... if we only follow the way that they operate and see the divine working of the universe... if we submit to the worship of their gods and spirits... that this is the way that we will obtain power and walk the way of the witch.

What Gianmichael offers is a different path and different way, one that is rooted in the Southern Italian Tradition, with roots in a lived and seasoned family tradition, and connection to the spiritual paths of antiquity; but this is a path that is meant to awaken in us the sense of our own true power and our own true nature.

It is one that is meant to connect us to the network of all the living and the dead, and to connect us to the true source of power and the boundless ebb and flow of energy of the planet and the cosmos.

And most importantly this practice will connect us to our ancestry, and the roots from which we come -- both of blood and of spirit; and it is from these roots that we will draw from the well of our own authenticity coming from the past and can spur and move us on into the future.

I am an adoptee of the Southern Italian Magical Tradition, being something that I learned from my first mentor that I had met while discerning Catholic religious life, this would lead me to adopt Catholic folk magic and Conjure as my own magical path. It wasn't until I met Gianmichael that many of the principles I learned came and were tied together into a cohesive practice, with both form and philosophical application united.

What Gianmichael taught me that the Italian magical path is a path that is open to those who are called to it, and that the principles therein are ones that can be applied to all magical practice across the board.

It is about applying the principles, doing the work, and connecting into ancestral wisdom that allows our practice to bloom and flourish.

Many times (especially in pop culture witchcraft circles) we are given a list of formulas to follow and spells, step-by-step instruction of what to do. We become clones of someone else's work and tradition, but we are never given the why. We are never given in many cases the practical information, of why or how magic works that we can break free of the formula to truly make the magic and the craft our own.

What we have been offered in these pages is the liberation to claim our magic and grab it by the horns! What we are given is the permission that we need to break away from pure conformity and performance and walk our own magical path.

Magic is about family.

What I mean by that is that magic wells up from the connection we form with our ancestors as Gianmichael so eloquently states in these pages.

Magic begins first and foremost with the connections to our ancestors of blood, spirit, place, tribe, etc. -- the wells of ancestral wisdom that we have to draw from which knows no end.

Once we begin to drink from those ancestral wells, we will come to know our true vocations and the way that we are to serve our communities and the world.

In many ways I think in our modern spiritual culture we have become very solitary and selfish.

It is about *my* magic, *my* growth; it is about *my* betterment (and in a way this is true); but the way that we get there is not one of navel gazing at our own life and fulfillment, it is recognizing our interconnectedness with each other, and the universe around us that brings us into our fulfillment.

It is not something that we can completely do by ourselves; we come to know the fullness of our magic by being in family, and within community with each other, the spirits we work with, our ancestors and with the cosmos.

It is not until we develop this familial connection with each other that we truly understand how powerful our magic is, and how that magic is meant to not only transform our own lives, but the lives of those around us, and therefore we transform each other.

What Gianmichael has done for me in my magical path has been to invite me into his spiritual family and legacy, and has gifted me with many siblings through the Inner Alchemy Mystery School.

We are a family of practitioners. We are here to learn and support each other in our growth. Through the sharing of the wisdom of this book, Gianmichael offers you this same invitation that he has offered to all of us. He invites you to sit down at the kitchen table, to eat with us and draw from the wells of wisdom… to be family with us and to be in community with us.

This is an invitation to awaken magic that is bigger than ourselves and has the power to reshape the whole of humanity, bringing all back into community with each other. I hope and encourage you to answer this invitation and to join us at the table.

Michael Therese McQueen

**Writer, Teacher, Mystic,
Catholic conjure practitioner, Witch**

Resources

- Inner Alchemy Mystery School
  www.InnerAlchemy.online

- The Contemplative Order of Compassion
  www.ContemplativeOrderOfCompassion.org

- Contact the author on social media
  www.StregaMystica.com

Other Books by the Author

- Magick at the Crossroads: Italian Folk Magic & the Old Religion
- The Magic of Forgiveness
- Zenkondo: Living from a Place of Primordial Boundless Compassion
- Mental Mastery: The Alchemy of the Magical Mind
- The Wisdom of Donald Trump (parody)

Previously released titles under the author's monastic name (Gurudas Sunyatananda)

- Sunyata
- Seven-Pointed Mind Mastery
- The Dharma of Compassion
- Awakening the Dharma of Compassion
- Tea & Dharma

Made in the USA
Middletown, DE
22 April 2023

29320156R00137